Looking at Birds

and

Considering Lilies

Written by William M. Schwein

ISBN 978-0-578-97991-5

Illustrations by Carol Baird

For Sharon, constant companion--
communing with nature, watching birds
and tending flowers.

Contents

Part One
Looking at Birds

Part Two
Considering Lilies

Author's Note

About the only things Jesus told us to do that I perform faithfully and passionately are looking at birds and considering flowers. Ever since my childhood, when I helped Grandpa Schwein in his greenhouse, I have loved working in a garden. As a result of my grandfather's mentoring, I planted store-bought flowers in every bare space around my first parsonage. At my second church, I decided to start flower seeds in the winter. At every church since, my goal was to make the parsonage yard look better than when we came.

When I was a teen-ager, I became a life member of the Indiana Audubon Society. I've watched them, fed them, counted them, studied them. Just in our own back yard (wooded, near a creek), we've counted nearly 50 species. They entertain and enlighten us daily.

Jesus spent a lot of time outside. Not surprising then, many of his parables were agrarian, horticultural and ornithological. Jesus didn't mean for us all to become botanists or birdwatchers. He simply taught that there were profound theological insights to be gained from paying attention to what was in the ground and in the air. To counteract the worries of those who listened to him, he used birds and fields of wildflowers as illustrations of how God provides.

This book grew out of two series of sermons: "Considering the Birds of the Air" and "In the Garden." I pray that what I've learned might provide a few life lessons for you.

William Schwein

Acknowledgements

Writing a book is like sowing seeds—then asking others to help tend the garden. My sincerest thanks to Bob and Brenda Warne, Sharon Hobson, and John Longworth (who prepared the manuscript for submission) for being my Master Gardeners. Also, thanks to John James Audubon and Grandpa Schwein.

As Søren Kierkegaard wrote in *The Lily of the Field and the Bird of the Air: Three Godly Discourses,* "And even if what you want to accomplish in the world were the most amazing feat: you shall acknowledge the lily and the bird as your teachers…"

Part One
Looking at Birds

1. Bluebirds

Read Psalm 128

According to Ben, Cathryn, and John Sill, there are any number of unique birds I could write about. In their book, *Another Field Guide to Little-known & Seldom-Seen Birds of North* America, they describe the Duffer Shank, which is found on "large grassy areas with occasional wooded borders, and whose egg is a small white sphere with a dimpled appearance." The Yellow-bellied Prairie Chicken, which is known for backing away from confrontations and retreating from about everything. The Crosscut Sawbill, found in deep woods. Blue Darts, which are perfectly camouflaged and attack flying insects from out of the blue. Greater Wandering Vagrants, which don't migrate, but just wander over much of North America before returning somewhere south in the fall. The Greater Noxious Grossbird, which leaves a ring around their dust bath.[1]

Unfortunately, I have never seen any of those unique species. But I've observed a lot of Big-headed Nitwits. They are extremely abundant and some even roost in church sanctuaries.

It is widely believed the birds to which Jesus was referring in the Sermon on the Mount were *ravens*. That is because the instruction he gives in Matthew 6:26, "Look at the birds of the air," is more specific in

[1]Ben, Cathryn and John Sill, *Another Field Guide to Little-known & Seldom-seen Birds of North America*, (Atlanta: Peachtree Publishers, LTD, 1990), 14, 22, 30, 36, 46, 50.

Luke 12:24, "Consider the *ravens*..." Ravens, of course, are larger than crows, their cousins. Neither are among my favorites.

Some scientists suggest there may be as many as 20,000 species of birds in the world. In many cultures, they are highly symbolic and thought to have spiritual meanings. In the book, *Birds in Legend, Fable, and Folklore*, Ernest Ingersoll writes about many of the birds associated with Christ's death on the cross: A red crossbill attempted to pry the nails from Jesus' limbs. The European robin plucked away the thorns from the crown on Jesus. The swallow hovered over Jesus crying, "Cheer up! Cheer up!" The dove sat nearby in mourning.[2]

Beyond the sacred, we have attributed to birds much symbolism. Eagles express freedom and independence. The owl, though it carries supernatural significance to Native American people, often symbolizes death; to others, it stands for wisdom and knowledge. (You may know the nursery rhyme, "The Wise Old Owl.") Cranes represent immortality and longevity. Storks, of course, deliver babies and are viewed as symbols of new life. Blue jays, fearlessness. Hummingbirds, joy.

There is probably no bird that has more *meaning* attached to it than the bluebird. They are probably the most desired bird to have at our feeders or to take up residence in specially made houses. There is even a North American Bluebird Society. Henry David Thoreau wrote, "The bluebird carries the sky on his back." In his Journal he wrote: "The bluebird...is like a speck of clear blue sky seen near the end of a storm, reminding us of an ethereal region and a heaven which we had forgotten...The bluebird comes and with his warble drills the ice and sets free the rivers and ponds and frozen ground."[3]

Bluebirds certainly do remind us of "a heaven which we had forgotten." It's no wonder we have associated the bluebird with happiness. I discovered a play written early in the twentieth century called "The Bluebird," by the Belgian playwright and poet, Maurice Maeterlinck. In the play two children set out trying to find the "Bluebird of Happiness." That was probably the first time bluebirds were thought of as a symbol of what many of us are seeking in life.

[2]Ernest Ingersoll, *Birds in Legend, Fable, and Folklore*, (New York: Longmans, Green and Co., 1923), 112-114.
[3]Henry Thoreau, *The Writings of Henry David Thoreau*, Journal XII, (Boston and New York: Houghton Mifflin and Company, 1906), 5.

There is an old song entitled "Little Child," written by Wayne Shanklin, which begins, "Daddy dear, Daddy dear, is the world really round? Tell me where is the bluebird of happiness found?

Many of us would like to know the answer to *where is the bluebird of happiness found?* Apparently, Americans aren't too good at solving that one; we do not rank in the global top 10 of Happiest Countries (Finland wins).

Jesus told many parables which grew out of his instruction to consider the lilies of the field. But his other reference to nature--encouraging us to look at the birds of the air--to my knowledge, never led to a parable about the birds. He might have told one like this:

> There was a man who loved bluebirds and who wanted to keep them from becoming extinct, so he set up an area where he would encourage them to nest. He knew that because of urban sprawl and development, there were fewer and fewer nesting sites available to them. He also knew it would be a battle, because the house sparrows, chickadees and even house wrens would compete with the bluebirds for nesting sites. So, he placed a nesting box right by a meadow that had plenty of insects for them to eat. He was elated when the first pair of bluebirds came to check out the area in the spring. He was thrilled when they began to investigate the nest hole. The next few days, he was encouraged when they built a nest. And he grew even more encouraged when the female laid four clear blue eggs. But one day he looked inside the box and saw that the nest had been taken over by sparrows. And he went away sorrowful.

Sometimes when Jesus told a parable, his disciples would ask him to explain it. If that had happened, I think he would have said that in his story bluebirds represented happiness and the man's efforts to get them to nest were like the attempts we make in finding happiness and keeping it from becoming endangered or even extinct in our lives. The sparrows would be everything in life that keeps us from being happy. Happiness doesn't seem to stay very long, does it? And it always appears to be driven away by some force determined to steal it from us.

Shouldn't we be happier than we are? One expert on happiness reports that perhaps only about 20% of Americans are truly happy. Bobby McFerrin's song, "Don't Worry. Be Happy" sold 10 million copies. We have to remind ourselves to be happy, with all those Smiley Face stickers and t-shirts. In the words of a country-western song, "The happily we're ever after" is pretty elusive, isn't it? So much spoils our happiness—or never lets it come to life. Few life stories ever reach that "happily ever after" conclusion.

Over and over people will say, "I just want to be happy…in my job." "I want to be happy…in my marriage." I've known many people who, after suffering some kind of loss, ask themselves and others, "Will I ever be happy again?" There is a proverb in the book of Job that says "One dies in full prosperity, being wholly at ease and secure…Another dies in bitterness of soul, never having tasted of good" (Job 21:23-25). We are afraid we'll never taste all that's good in life.

I have read how Hollywood often meddles with a bestseller or a classic's ending to improve its chances at the box office. When the book didn't have a happy ending, the movie did. That happened with *Jurassic Park, Breakfast at Tiffany's, The Scarlet Letter,* among others. (In Hawthorne's novel, Reverend Dimmesdale dies; in the movie, he runs off with Hester Prynne.) We'd probably all like to think there's someone who can guarantee a happy ending to our life story.

The Bible doesn't use the word "happy" very often. It talks more about joy and contentment. But the very first Psalm begins, "Happy are those…" And the 128th Psalm begins "Happy is everyone who fears the Lord, who walks in his ways." We believe this psalm was originally a formal blessing for the pilgrims who had come to Jerusalem. The pilgrim was assured that their work would be fruitful, they'd be happy, things would go well for them, they'd have good fortune all their days, a man's wife would be like a fruitful vine and his children like olive shoots, he would see prosperity and live to see his grandchildren. But we know there are no guarantees that those promises came true.

I think one of the reasons we miss out on happiness is that we think it's a permanent state and not just a temporary experience. Those who observe bird behavior suggest that birds have a rather narrow awareness-span. Whereas humans are constantly aware of what's already gone on, and what may yet be, birds live in the present. We overload our minds with regrets from the past and fears for the future. The thoughts act like invasive sparrows when they push out opportunities for happiness in the present.

That reminds me of Robert Burns' poem to a mouse, in which he praises the little creature for only being concerned about present dangers:

Still thou art blest, compared wi' me!
The present only toucheth thee;
But, och! I backward cast my eye
On prospects drear!
An' forward though I canna see,
I guess an' fear![4]

Maybe we can learn from birds not to miss the moment. That's what we do. We spend a lot of time reviewing happy memories and looking ahead in expectation—and we are but dimly aware of the present, the here and now. In his marvelous book, *Celebrate the Temporary,* Clyde Reid writes that we should "Live in the now." I once heard that we should learn to live in "day-tight compartments."

Bob Raines has written that we "confuse duration with significance." We can't measure everything by length; depth is equally important. In one of William Blake's poems, "Eternity," he said, "He who kisses the joy as it flies, lives in eternity's sunrise." Kiss the joy as it flies. Ben Franklin wrote, "Happiness consists more in small pleasures that occur every day, than in great pieces of good fortune that happen but seldom in the course of life." That's why we can't hold on to some of what brings us pleasure; we just have to make sure we *behold* it. An expert on health and happiness has said that the things that make us happiest and healthiest are lots of life's small, everyday pleasures, not the rare peaks of ecstasy.

I began thinking about those small pleasures as I worked on this chapter--what I would call the *bluebird times* of our lives, those moments and momentary experiences that remind us life is good. (You might want to make up your own list.) Hearing your favorite song on the radio. Hot towels out of the dryer. Lying in bed listening to the rain outside. Playing with a new puppy. Swinging on a swing. Watching a really beautiful sunset. Having someone listen to you and then tell you that everything is going to be okay. Sitting outside and looking at the stars. Smelling the four o'clocks in the evening air. Seeing a goldfinch perched on the black-eyed Susan, eating the seeds. John Updike once called them the "uncaused moments of sheer grateful happiness" that he occasionally experienced.

The truth is, we overlook so much of what can bring us happiness, as fleeting as it might be. I love the story of Emily Dickinson's father, who,

[4]Robert Burns, *Poems, Chiefly in the Scottish Dialect.*

like his daughter, was sensitive to the beauty of the world. He was in the town square one evening when a glorious sunset began to develop. Discovering himself to be the only viewer of that marvel, and presuming his neighbors to be at their supper tables, he ran to the town fire bell and vigorously pulled the rope. When the townspeople appeared, and demanded to know the location of the fire, Dickinson pointed to the majestic panorama of color and design in the West.

Someone once said that if the stars came out only once a year, the whole world would go out and look at them. Maybe that's why the bluebird represents happiness for us. They aren't as common as starlings and sparrows. Nor are they as obvious. You have to keep an eye out to see them, perched on a fence or telephone wire. You have to be open and observant. I am always moved by that scene in Thornton Wilder's *Our Town* when Emily comes back from her grave in Grover's Corners cemetery and relives her twelfth birthday. She knows in that moment how much she had missed and how hard it was to know she would never return. She lamented, "Good-by to clocks ticking…and Mama's sunflowers. And food and coffee. And new-ironed dresses and hot baths…and sleeping and waking up. Oh, earth, you're too wonderful for anybody to realize you. Do any human beings ever realize life while they live it?—every, every minute?"[5]

Good question, isn't it?

Don't forget that the psalmist says, "This is the day that the Lord has made; let us rejoice and be glad in it" (Ps 118:24). Not the week or the month or the year that God makes and gives us—but the day. Eugene Peterson translates a verse from the Sermon on the Mount this way: "Give your entire attention to what God is doing right now" (Mt 6:24, *The Message*).[6] I have a friend who calls them life's "butterfly moments," like when a butterfly lands on our hand or a nearby flower. You can't make that happen. It just does.

I've noticed how skittish and elusive bluebirds are. We have had them come to our feeders (enjoying the mealworms), but they never allow us to approach them. Unlike the house finches and the chickadees, they are certainly not consistent in their visits.

Nathanael Hawthorne is mistakenly given credit for writing, "Happiness is like a butterfly which, when pursued, is always beyond our

[5]Thornton Wilder, *Our Town*, (Copyright The Wilder Family LLC, 1938), 65.
[6]Eugene Peterson, *The Message: New Testament with Psalms and Proverbs*, (Colorado Springs: NavPress, 1995), 24.

grasp, but, if you will sit down quietly, may alight upon you." It was actually written by J. Richard Lessor, a social worker, in the 1970s. What Hawthorne actually did write was, "Happiness in this world, when it comes, comes incidentally. Make it the object of pursuit, and it leads us on a wild goose chase, and is never attained. Follow some other object, and very possibly we may find that we have caught happiness without dreaming of it." Many of us think we can purchase happiness; too many of us also spend our lives pursuing it. Isn't it interesting that the *pursuit of happiness* is included with *life and liberty* in our Declaration of Independence? It may be a fundamental right, but as an ancient Chinese philosopher said, "Happiness is the absence of striving for happiness."

I had a good friend who was a cardiologist and a bird-watcher. He did a lot to save the bluebirds in the greater Indianapolis area. Bluebirds have so many enemies, including other birds, and urban sprawl. He and I spent one Memorial Day checking nine bluebird houses on some vacant farmland. He told me later someone with a paintball gun had destroyed one of the boxes and killed the baby bluebirds in it. Much later, he sent me an e-mail copy of a letter he had written to his son, who helped him look after what they call a "bluebird trail."

Dear Danny,

I went to the trail today. At Box 1, I found that all the swallows' eggs had been pecked open and thrown out of the box. I knew that was the work of wrens. They were taking over the trail. Sure enough, there was a wren nest in every single box thereafter, except 6, where the 5 little chickadees were in full feather. They scrunched down and scowled up at me. When I got to 9, I feared the worst. Our 5 baby bluebirds should have been about to fledge. This was the one time we knew we were not supposed to open the box to check on them because we might frighten them and make them leave before they were ready. So, I stood and watched and listened for 10 minutes. I knew--that if they were about to fledge, that they would be noisy, and their parents would be busily flying in and out to feed them. I knew if they had already fledged, that they would be in the nearby apple tree yapping for food until they learned to fly. But I heard

nothing, and I saw nothing. So carefully, I opened the box. My heart sank. The nest had been demolished. It was wet and rotting from last night's rain. I dropped to my knees and started searching the ground around the box to see if I could find the babies. Nothing. Only poison ivy. I felt like crying. I walked slowly back to the car hoping I might find them somewhere, but I didn't. I got in the car and drove off toward the road. Through the sunroof I thought I heard a soft little off-key bluebird call. I figured it was my imagination, but I got out and walked toward the hackberry by the fencerow where the sound had come from. There they were, all five of them, flitting about from branch to branch, fuzzy, carefree, and curious about who this stranger was in a white shirt and tie looking at them with tears in his eyes.

Questions for Contemplating and Conversing

1. When were you the happiest in your life?
2. Was it the result of external circumstances or an inner attitude?
3. Have you *pursued* happiness? Is it one of your life goals?
4. What would it take to make you happier?
5. Why do you think the United States is not the happiest country in the world?
6. The unofficial nickname for Disneyland is "The Happiest Place on Earth." Why would the Disney organization make that claim? Would you agree with their assessment? Why or Why not?
7. Do you have a location that might be your "happiest place on earth?"
8. What are the contributors to our happiness?
9. What is the main lesson you learned from this chapter?

2. Eagles

Read Deuteronomy 32:10-12

I remember very few sermons I have ever heard. (Even fewer that I have preached.) Most are not memorable. But I do recall a sermon a friend preached maybe fifty years ago. Honestly, I don't remember the sermon, just the text from the book of Proverbs:

> Three things are too wonderful for me;
> four I do not understand:
> the way of an eagle in the sky,
> the way of a snake on a rock,
> the way of a ship on the high seas,
> and the way of a man with a girl. (Prov 30:18-19)

I think I know a little about snakes on a rock. I used to collect them as a kid. I usually had a basement full of snake cages. I don't understand much about sailing, or how ships can stay afloat on the ocean. Like most men, I have absolutely no understanding of "the way of a man with a girl." And I can't help but be amazed by the way of an eagle in the sky.

Have you ever watched one of those magnificent birds soaring in the heavens? Some of them can reach 30 miles an hour without ever flapping their wings, riding on the thermals that rise from the earth. No craft we can design is as maneuverable. They fly for hours with only the slightest movement of their wings, gliding in harmony with the air. They have been spotted as high as 10,000 feet and can dive at speeds of 100 mph.

They are intelligent, proud. It's no wonder they caught the attention of biblical writers. Golden eagles are the largest flying bird found in Palestine, with a wingspan of eight feet. The sweep of their flight and the swiftness of their movement was so fascinating they were considered the noblest of the birds. They also became a symbol for God. In Exodus, God tells Moses to remind the Israelites that when God brought them out of Egypt, God bore them "on eagles' wings" (Ex 19:4). That metaphor is repeated in Deuteronomy. In the Song of Moses, about God's faithfulness, God's saving deeds are recited. God had protected the Israelites during their wilderness wanderings. "As an eagle stirs up its nest, and hovers over its young; as it spreads its wings, takes them up, and bears them aloft on its pinions, the Lord alone guided" them (Deut 32:11-12). A parent eagle watches the young almost constantly. One adult is at or right next to the nest, feeding them, sheltering them from the elements. That same care continues as the young leave the nest and set out on their own. That's the same way God cared for the children of Israel; shielding them, guarding them, protecting them.

Eagle nests are in inaccessible high places. Most are made in the tallest trees, sometimes over 100 feet high. (Both male and female bald eagles help build the nest, which might be a good reminder to most fathers. Dads are homemakers too.) When a mother eagle builds her nest, she starts with thorns, broken branches, sharp rocks, and a number of other items that seem entirely unsuitable for the project. The nests can be six feet in diameter and four feet deep. Eagles have been known to carry odd objects such as light bulbs, trash, and string to the nest. Eagles returning for a second year often build right on top of the previous year's nest. One nest was estimated to weigh two tons. Then the mother lines the nest with a thick padding of moss, wool, feathers, and fur from animals she has killed, making it soft and comfortable for the eggs.[1] By the time the growing birds reach flying age, the comfort of the nest and the luxury of free meals make them quite reluctant to leave. According to legend, that's when the mother eagle begins "stirring up the nest." I've also heard that the mother puts an eaglet on her back and soars upward as high as she can fly. She then turns upside down and the baby eaglet starts falling off. Most of the time they just start flying, but if one doesn't get the hang of it, the mother

[1] Donald and Lillian Stokes, *A Guide to Bird Behavior Volume 3*, (Boston: Little, Brown and Company, 1989), 90-91.

eagle will swoop down, pick the eaglet out of the air and repeat the maneuver until the young bird learns to fly. Ornithologists say that's just not true, though it's wonderful to imagine.

More accurately, the mother eagles "entice" the young to leave the nest. They coax them, rather than shove them. They swoop by the nest with food, staying distanced. The fledgling gets hungry and ventures out of the nest. Eagles do not teach the young to fly; they fly around the nest and challenge them with an example to be emulated.

Likewise, most of the powerful and positive experiences we have in life begin with some kind of risk-taking, like leaving the nest.

There are times in our lives when God has to "stir up our nest," but at the same time God "hovers over us," and "bears us on eagle's wings." Sometimes, in a sense, the "soft moss" is removed from our nests (or the padding from the church pews) so that we begin to feel the urge and urgency to move out and learn to soar. I think there are times when God is behind that. As we like to say, God afflicts the comfortable just as often as God comforts the afflicted. When Alan Paton saw his son growing up, he wrote these lines for him,

I see my son is wearing long trousers, I tremble at this…
Go forward, eager and reverent child, see here
I begin to take my hands away from you…
(Life) lies in wait for you, she cannot but hurt you;
Go forward, go forward, I hold the bandages
and ointments ready…[2]

God never sends us out without promising to go with us.

I remember the first time I heard (and sang) "On Eagle's Wings." It was at a Marriage Renewal Ceremony. It has become one of my favorite hymns. It is globally popular. The composer, Father Jan Michael Joncas, wrote it after a friend's father had died. He said he just wanted to "create something that would be both prayerful and then comforting." Since then, it has been used at funerals, and was featured at the memorial for those killed in the bombing of the Federal Building in Oklahoma City. President-elect Biden quoted it during his first speech as president-elect. Whenever it is sung, it touches people's hearts, especially in times of grief and pain.

[2]Alan Paton, *Meditation for a Young Boy Confirmed*, (United Kingdom: S.P.C.K., 1959), 13.

And God will raise you up on eagle's wings,
Bear you on the breath of dawn,
Make you to shine like the sun,
And hold you in the palm of God's hand.[3]

I'd guess most all of us are familiar with the poem, *Footprints*, by Margaret Fishback. (The authorship of the poem is disputed.) She dreamed she was walking along the beach with God. She looked back at the footprints left in the sand. She saw only one set of footprints, during the lowest and saddest times of her life. She asked God about it, and God whispered to her:

My precious child,
I love you and will never leave you
never, ever, during your trials and testings.
When you saw only one set of footprints
it was then that I carried you.[4]

There are times when God carries us.

There is a second reference to the eagle that may speak to us. An unknown poet wrote:

Lord, I don't mean to complain, but I'm tired,
tired of having to be the strong one,
tired of never getting everything
done that needs doing.
The calendar says my body is a few decades old.
I feel it. But on the inside I'm still a little child,
a little child in need of my
Father's comfort and strength.
Help me to draw upon your strength,
to feel your strong arms holding me up.
"My little child, I know how tired you are.
I see that your reservoir of strength

[3]Jan Michael Joncas, "On Eagle's Wings," (Phoenix, North American Liturgy Resources, 1979).
[4]Margaret Fishback Powers, *Footprints: The True Story Behind the Poem That Inspired Millions*. (New York: HarperCollins, 2012), 252.

is temporarily low.
Fortunately for you,
mine never is.
My strength is perfect
when your strength is gone.
Come to me and rest awhile.
Breathe deeply of my energizing flow of life…
You will come through your time of weariness,
not only strengthened but encouraged,
knowing that I have strengthened you
with power through my Spirit."

Even strong mothers can feel like a little child on the inside, in need of a Heavenly Father's comfort and strength. At least the smart ones do. The really smart ones know that "Even youths will faint and be weary, and the young will fall exhausted…" but that "those who wait for the Lord shall renew their strength, they shall mount up with wings like eagles…" (Isa 40:30-31).

The eagle is a symbol of renewable energy. Biblical writers believed that an eagle renews its strength and youthful appearance after shedding its feathers. The psalmist said that God "satisfies you with good as long as you live so that your youth is renewed like the eagle's" (Ps 103:5).

A man went into a hardware store carrying a chain saw. He threw the saw down at the clerk's feet and said, "This is a piece of junk. You told me that I could cut down forty trees a day, and I couldn't cut down any more than three." The clerk replied, "Well, maybe the teeth on the saw need to be sharpened." When they had sharpened the saw, the man took the saw back home. He returned three days later with almost the same complaint: "This is still a piece of junk. It's a little bit better, but not much. Now I can cut down only five trees a day, and you said I could cut down forty. I really want my money back this time." "I really don't understand it," replied the clerk. "This is a good piece of equipment. Let me try it." So, he pulled the starter cord and the chain saw started right up. The man looked at it, surprised, and said, "What in the world is that noise?"

Too many of us are like that. We push our riding mowers. We've never used the power. God's power is our greatest resource. We of all people should know that. The key is to wait on and depend upon God. Max

Lucado has said, "It's much easier to raise the sail than row the boat."[5] We neglect a wonderful source of power.

Baptist preacher John Claypool said that when we look to God and depend upon God, we will be given strength from Beyond. Claypool describes three ways that strength can come to us: as ecstasy, "to mount up with wings as eagles;" as energy, "to run and not be weary;" and as endurance, "to walk and not faint." When there is no ecstasy, no great burst of energy, there is at least the gift of endurance. He says that some commentators have questioned the sequence of Isaiah's process: it should have been the other way around—endurance the least significant, then energy, and finally the climax of ecstasy. Walk, run and then soar. Claypool said that an experience of personal suffering (his young daughter's death) taught him that Isaiah understood human need: the hardest challenges in life come not at the point of strength, but at the point of helplessness and weakness.

> What is more difficult, I ask you, than trying "to keep on keeping on" when you find yourself surrounded by immensities you cannot change and when there is nothing to do except hold on and try to endure? When there is no occasion to soar and no place to run, then the promise of strength "to walk and not faint," small as it may seem, becomes infinitely significant and appropriate; in fact, it is the best gift of all.[6]

The third lesson we might learn from looking at the eagle is best illustrated by a story.

> A certain man went through a forest seeking any bird of interest he might find. He caught a young eagle, brought it home and put it among his fowls and ducks and turkeys, and gave it chickens' food to eat even though it was an eagle, the king of birds. Five years later a naturalist came to see him and, after passing through his garden, said: "That bird is an eagle, not a chicken.'" "Yes," said its owner, "but I have trained it to be a chicken. It is no longer an eagle, it is a chicken, even though it measures

[5] Max Lucado, *A Gentle Thunder: Hearing God Through the Storm*. (United States: Thomas Nelson, 2012), 63.

[6] John Claypool, *Tracks of a Fellow Struggler: Living and Growing through Grief*, (Harrisburg, PA: Morehouse Publishing, 2004 edition).

fifteen feet from tip to tip of its wings." "No," said the naturalist, "it is an eagle still: it has the heart of an eagle, and I will make it soar high up to the heavens." "No," said the owner, "it is a chicken, and it will never fly." They agreed to test it. The naturalist picked up the eagle, held it up, and said with great intensity, "Eagle, thou art an eagle; thou dost belong to the sky and not to this earth; stretch forth thy wings and fly." The eagle turned this way and that, and then, looking down, saw the chickens eating their food, and down he jumped. The owner said: "I told you it was a chicken." "No,' said the naturalist, "it is an eagle. Give it another chance tomorrow." So the next day he took it to the top and the house and said: "Eagle, thou art an eagle; stretch forth thy wings and fly." But again the eagle, seeing the chickens feeding, jumped down and fed with them. Then the owner said: "I told you it was a chicken." "No," asserted the naturalist, "it is an eagle, and it still has the heart of an eagle; only give it one more chance, and I will make it fly tomorrow." The next morning he rose early and took the eagle outside the city, away from the houses, to the foot of a high mountain. The sun was just rising, gilding the top of the mountain with gold, and every crag was glistening in the joy of that beautiful morning. He picked up the eagle and said to it: "Eagle, thou art an eagle; thou dost belong to the sky and not to this earth; stretch forth thy wings and fly!" The eagle looked around and trembled as if new life were coming to it; but it did not fly. The naturalist then made it look straight at the sun. Suddenly it stretched out its wings and, with the screech of an eagle, it mounted higher and higher and never returned. It was an eagle, though it had been kept and tamed as a chicken![7]

I think a lot of us have learned to think of ourselves as something we aren't, but we can decide in favor of becoming who we really are. Many of us find ourselves in a chicken yard feeling comfortable, but with no sense of life in all its abundance. We have adopted a chicken philosophy of life. But we are really eagles with the potential to soar!

The French poet, Antoine de Saint-Exupéry, wrote in his book, *Wind, Sand and Stars*:

[7] James Aggrey, *Eagle Would Not Fly*, (Pakistan Fitzhenry & Whiteside, Limited, 1988).

> I looked about me. Luminous points glowed in the darkness. Cigarettes punctuated the humble meditations of worn old clerks. I heard them talking to one another in murmurs and whispers. They talked about illness, money, shabby domestic cares. And suddenly I had a vision of the face of destiny. Old bureaucrat, my comrade, it is not you who are to blame. No one ever helped you to escape. You, like a termite, built your peace by blocking up with cement every chink and cranny through which the light might pierce. You rolled yourself up into a ball in your genteel security, in routine, in the stifling conventions of provincial life, raising a modest rampart against the winds and the tides and the stars. You have chosen not to be perturbed by great problems, having trouble enough to forget your own fate as a man. You are not the dweller upon an errant planet and do not ask yourself questions to which there are no answers. Nobody grasped you by the shoulder while there was still time. Now the clay of which you were shaped has dried and hardened, and naught in you will ever awaken the sleeping musician, the poet, the astronomer that possibly inhabited you in the beginning.[8]

Many of us just might be chickens with an eagle sleeping, hiding and residing inside of us; just waiting to be challenged or permitted to become who we really are. God may be stirring up the nest in which you have grown complacent. This may be the time you are to "mount up with wings like the eagle." If it is, remember that God will be with you to be the wind beneath your wings.

Questions for Contemplating and Conversing

1. What did you think the first time you saw an eagle?
2. The bald eagle has been the national bird of the United States since 1782. It appears on the Great Seal of our country. It is said to be the most pictured bird in all of America. One of the opponents of the idea of the bald eagle's prominence was

[8] Antoine de Saint-Exupéry, *Wind, Sand and Stars*, (New York: Reynal & Hitchcock, 1939), 11.

Benjamin Franklin. He wrote to a friend: "I wish the bald eagle had not been chosen as the representative of our country; he is a bird of bad moral character; like those among men who live by sharping and robbing, he is generally poor, and often very lousy. The turkey is a much more respectable bird and withal a true, original native of America." Much later, President John F. Kennedy wrote to the Audubon Society: "The Founding Fathers made an appropriate choice when they selected the bald eagle as the emblem of the nation. The fierce beauty and proud independence of this great bird aptly symbolizes the strength and freedom of America. But as latter-day citizens we shall fail our trust if we permit the eagle to disappear."

3. How do you feel about the bald eagle as our national bird? Are there others that might be more appropriate? Turkeys?
4. When have you felt like a *chicken* and wanted to be more like an *eagle?*
5. What wearies you the most?
6. Have you ever experienced God as a "second wind"?
7. What is the main lesson you learned from this chapter?

3. Geese

Read I Corinthians 12:14-27

The whole point of this book is to increase your power of observation, to be more in touch and in tune with our Father's World, and to look for lessons to be learned from watching the birds. We can feel a kindship with God's creatures. For many of us, that was never more memorable than the first time we heard and saw Canada geese high above us as they migrated.

Even those of us who are oblivious to everything else around or above us probably remember stopping to witness the migration of Canada geese. I know they don't do that much anymore, having become year-round residents, but there is probably no other bird that has more to teach us than geese. We still occasionally see them flying in the familiar V-formation—usually just hurrying to another feeding area or one of the golf courses in the area. I read somewhere that they have become the bane of every golf course manager's existence. The problem is that everywhere the geese go, the geese "go." And the real problem is that they no longer go anywhere. They stay. And they stay together. Canada geese remain paired for as long as both live. I read the other day about a pair of geese that had chosen a nesting spot located close to a road. A few days after laying her eggs, the female wandered into the path of a car. Luckily, she only suffered a broken leg. But while she was taken to a veterinary clinic and admitted into a recovery ward, her faithful mate was left alone to tend their nest. The male not only continued to do all the nest sitting; he also established a unique "coffee break" ritual for himself. When he would leave the nest to eat and drink, he would return by way of the road where his mate was injured. Then he settled down and patiently waited for his wounded mate to reappear, only reluctantly making his way back to his solitary incubation duties from time to time.

We can learn a lot from watching individual birds, but there is something also to be learned from watching how they get along together. I've always been fascinated by the way some species of birds *flock*. A few years ago, I saw a couple dozen cedar waxwings in the top of a dead tree in a neighbor's yard. Robins flock together, some of them migrating, others staying in groups of fifty to one hundred birds throughout the winter. Black-capped chickadees form small flocks of six to ten birds. Grackles gather in the thousands, making for spectacular formations in flight.

Nothing is more fascinating to me in the behavior of birds than their seasonal movements, their migratory patterns. It is still a mystery how they find their way over vast distances with such apparent ease. Some scientists believe they fly by means of visual landmarks like river valleys or mountains. Others say they use the sun as a compass, or it is the bird's response to the earth's magnetic field. One shore bird flew 1,900 miles from Cape Cod to Martinique in six days. The arctic tern travels 10,000 miles in late summer. Storks summer in Europe but spend the winter in South Africa. Among land birds, the bobolink is the top migrant, covering 7,000 miles or more between the clover fields of Canada and the grasslands of Argentina.

People of faith would like to think that God has a hand in all that. One of the earliest bits of poetry I was taught was William Cullen Bryant's "To A Waterfowl."

> He who, from zone to zone,
> Guides through the boundless sky thy certain flight,
> In the long way that I must tread alone,
> Will lead my steps aright.

What some call instinct, others would call divine guidance. In the book of Job, God takes credit for the wisdom behind the hawk that "spreads its wings toward the south" (Job 39:26).

I think there is a significant lesson we can learn from geese. But before we get into that, I want to acknowledge what authorities on bird behavior, Don and Lillian Stokes, caution against in one of their books. They write,

Although behavior-watching can produce insights into human behavior, applying human motives to birds can be very limiting. When most of us try to supply motives for the behavior of animals, we invariably use motives that we would have in the same situation. "The bird scolded me." "The mother bird was teaching its young how to fly." "He sang happily from his perch." All of these statements are anthropomorphic: they are assumptions about the motives of birds based on human values. This tendency to explain the actions of birds in human terms greatly limits our ability to learn new things about the avian world…What a bird does and why it does it are two different things.[1]

Having acknowledged the dangers of making animals into more than the creatures they are, it's still true that sometimes they behave more humanely than we do. Dolphins, for example, build strong family ties, recognize the benefits of the sense of touch, protect each other from sharks, care for the weak and wounded, learn to listen, cultivate a win-win lifestyle, and have a "go with the flow" flexibility. They have a lot to teach us about relating to one another.

But geese are perhaps the greatest teachers in human relations. I think I first became aware of that on a retreat some years back. I don't remember who the leader was, but she distributed a sheet titled "A Lesson from the Geese":

> **Fact 1** As each goose flaps its wings it creates an "uplift" for the birds that follow. By flying in a "V" formation, the whole flock adds 71% greater flying range than if each bird flew alone.
> **Lesson 1** People who share a common direction and sense of community can get where they are going quicker and easier because they are traveling on the thrust of one another.
> **Fact 2** When a goose falls out of formation, it suddenly feels the drag and resistance of flying alone. It quickly moves back into formation to take advantage of the lifting power of the bird in front of it.
> **Lesson 2** If we have as much common sense as a goose, we stay in formation with those headed where we want to go. We are willing to accept their help and give our help to others.

[1] Donald Stokes, *A Guide to Bird Behavior Volume I*, (Boston: Little, Brown and Company, 1979), 5

Fact 3 When the lead goose tires, it rotates back into the formation and another goose flies to the point position.
Lesson 3 It pays to take turns doing the hard tasks and sharing leadership. As with geese, people are interdependent on each other's skills, capabilities, and unique arrangements of gifts, talents, or resources.
Fact 4 Geese flying in formation honk to encourage those up front to keep up their speed.
Lesson 4 We need to make sure our honking is encouraging. In groups where there is encouragement, the production is much greater. The power of encouragement (to stand by one's heart or core values and encourage the heart and core of others) is the quality of honking we seek.
Fact 5 When a goose gets sick, wounded, or shot down, two geese drop out of formation and follow it down to help protect it. They stay with it until it dies or is able to fly again. Then, they launch out with another formation or catch up with the flock.
Lesson 5 If we have as much sense as geese, we will stand by each other in difficult times as well as when we are strong.[2]

Browne Barr has taken all those lessons we can learn from geese and put them into a marvelous little book on the church and its ministry, *High-flying Geese.* He reminds us that Christians cannot fulfill their spiritual obligations in solitude. We cannot survive on our own. We need to be joined together in some sort of "flock." Like many other species of birds, geese have an instinct for creating communal life. We believe they simply enjoy each other's company. They congregate. We are fond of saying "birds of a feather flock together." That's why we have congregations. I looked up the definition of "gaggle" and learned a gaggle is a flock of geese when not in flight. I guess we don't become a true *flock* until we are airborne. It's like the difference between a group and a team. Just because a group of people meets together, it doesn't mean they will accomplish anything; they have to become a goal-oriented *team.* Probably the most obvious trait of geese is how they fly in formation. I wish we could learn to fly in formation in our churches. We mostly fly in most

[2] Transcribed from a speech given by Angeles Arrien at the 1981 Organizational Development Network and is based on the work of Milton Olson.

every direction. We could do better in accentuating our communal life and flying in formation as a flock.

The formation flight of birds improves aerodynamic efficiency. They fly faster in formation than one by one. Barr says, "The church is a formation, and when that is ignored, it does not even crawl very fast, much less fly!" Formation, structure, and order are necessary for the survival of the church. We won't last long if everyone just does his or her own thing. That says something about our need to worship together, to study together, and to meet in small discipleship or accountability groups. There is the need for tradition, ritual, and structure if we are to retain our identity. I understand geese have a takeoff ceremony. Before they are about to take off after having settled down on the ground for a while, they encourage one another, offering a kind of preflight support system. Experienced observers can even tell whether they intend a short flight or a long one by their movements. I sometimes wonder if worship shouldn't be our "preflight, takeoff ceremony." A church is doing what it was created to do when it is going somewhere. Worship is the time we're down here on the ground, encouraging one another, offering support to those who are trying to live out their Christianity through the week.[3]

Geese, flying in formation, also teach us the importance of sharing the lead. Or sharing the load. These are extremely challenging times for recruiting volunteers. In an essay that has generated a great deal of interest, *Bowling Alone,* Robert Putnam shows that there is a serious decline in what he calls "civic engagement." We don't bowl in organized leagues and we don't participate as much in a variety of civic arenas: politics, churches, labor unions, parent-teacher organizations and fraternal organizations. We don't sign petitions, run for public office, attend public meetings, serve as an officer or committee member in any local clubs or organizations, attend religious service, socialize informally with friends or neighbors, attend club meetings, join unions, entertain friends at home, participate in picnics, eat the evening meal with the whole family, send greeting cards, work on community projects, or give blood. The reasons? Putnam says it's due to a lot of things: generational change, television watching, suburbanization--with its associated increases in sprawl and commuting time, the pressures of time and money and the increase in two-

[3] Browne Barr, *High Flying Geese: Unexpected Reflections on the Church and Its Ministry*, (United States: Seabury Press, 1983).

career families.[4] One of the most critical needs in our church is to increase the number of persons who are involved in our ministry and mission. If we use Paul's analogy of the church as the body of Christ, our "body" is mostly ineffective or inactive. If your body were that impaired, you would probably be confined to a wheelchair as a paraplegic. In the church, we are too often paralyzed.

In order to involve persons, of course, we have to go against the prevailing mood of society today, which is rugged individualism. Too many of us operate as if Christianity were a golf game and not a team sport. Golfers are by nature independent. You rely on your own abilities to beat the others. Success in other sports, football, basketball, volleyball, and soccer, depends upon each player doing his own thing but working with other team members to accomplish something together. I read of a high school football coach who said it was increasingly difficult to get kids to come out for team sports, while club sports—like golf and track and tennis and swimming—are incredibly successful. They require individual effort, training, and preparation. You take *private* lessons to learn to do those things. They use their gifts for *personal* success.

Early in the twelfth chapter of I Corinthians, Paul affirms that to each one the manifestation of the Spirit is given "for the common good." That is absolutely crucial to our understanding of the church. The gifts we have are not for our own use alone, but are to be used for something greater than ourselves. I think it's that whole concept of "the common good" that we are in danger of losing. In his letter to the Ephesians, Paul says that God gave us gifts "to equip the saints for the work of ministry, for building up the body of Christ" (Eph 4:12).

Geese don't just fly along on their own. They look after one another. I would guess most of us turn our attention to geese flying in formation because we hear them honking. They "honk from behind." They are not complaining, like their human counterparts. Nor are they honking like we do our horns when we grow impatient at a stoplight. What they are doing is offering encouragement. It's the means by which they keep in touch and alert one another to danger. By changes in modulation and pitch and frequency they have a vocal network of mutuality and encouragement. We have a long way to go in the church before we fulfill the biblical affirmation that we are "members one of another." Some of you can no longer just stand by and watch your brothers and sisters burn themselves

[4] Robert D. Putnam, "Bowling Alone: America's Declining Social Capital," Journal of Democracy, January 1995, 65-78.

out. Geese, we observe, stand by each other. Most folks in the church just stand around.

Questions for Contemplating and Conversing

1. How do you feel about the fact that Canada geese don't seem to migrate south anymore?
2. Have you ever had an unpleasant encounter with a goose?
3. Have you taken the time to watch birds migrate? What did you think at the time?
4. Are there times, as humans, we should do a better job of "flying in formation"?
5. Has "rugged individualism" cost us a sense of community and the common good?
6. What is the main lesson you learned from this chapter?

4. Doves

Read Genesis 8:6-12; Luke 3:21-22

If the bluebird is associated with happiness, we might note that the mourning dove is immortalized by a woodworking method called *dovetailing.* Two pieces of wood are fit together with interlocking sides. If they are trapezoidal in shape, the joint resembles the tail feathers of a dove. (Dovetailing also applies to how other things fit together nicely, united closely, like when your plans coincide with your partner's plans.)

Birds are not just fun to look at; they are fascinating to study. For instance, most species of birds have incredible parenting skills, or instincts. Human parents can grow tired of having their children at home for an extended period. But bird parents have it tough, too. Baby birds require from one half to their full body weight of food each day. (It probably seems like that for those who have growing boys at home!) Both parent birds have to work from early morning until dark to keep up the supply of food. A house wren was observed to feed its young 1,217 times in 15 hours and 45 minutes. A pair of chickadees fed their young 40 times in 30 minutes.

Something else that impresses us about birds is how they defend their young. No matter how large the enemy may be, the parents will drive or lead the enemy away. One spring our son, Bill, came into the house to tell us he had found a baby robin on the ground. I put on a glove and went out to pick up the fledgling—to get it out of the way of our dog. About the time I reached down for it, seemingly out of nowhere, about half a dozen robins started their short, shrill calls and then started coming after me. I know one of them was the mother and I assume one of them was the father; maybe the others were just friends from the neighborhood.

When I began doing research into the behavior of mourning doves, I discovered an interesting fact. Male and female mourning doves share in the incubation of the eggs. The male incubates the eggs without once leaving the nest from morning until evening, and the female does the same from evening until morning. The changeover takes place between 8:30 and 10:30 in the morning and between 4:30 and 5:30 in the evening. (I know parents of infants who wish they could work out that kind of routine.) One other fascinating bit of information about the mourning dove: The male selects the nesting site. He also gathers the nesting material. He finds some twigs on the ground, sorts through them, selects one that he carries to the female. He perches next to her and gives her the piece, apparently seeking her approval. He then proceeds with making that rather loose, flat platform that doesn't do well in storms.[1]

We often see dove eggs on the ground. One reason is that their nests are a mess. Not very securely attached to a limb. What the doves fail in making their nests, they make up for in their devotion to offspring. When approached while sitting on the nest, they may fly off and pretend to be injured, as a distraction. I recall finding a dove's nest very low in the apple tree in our back yard. I was curious about what I would do if I attempted to come close to the nest. I slowly moved closer until I could reach out and touch the dove, and it sat there calmly as if to say, "No closer, buddy. I'm not moving."

Most birds are noticed for their songs and calls. Our attention is most likely drawn to doves when we hear the whistling sound made by their wings. When they take off, they flap their wings and the air rushing through the special flight feathers causes what is known as a *wing whistle.* It's both alarm and defensive measure. They also clap their wings together when they lift into flight.

We also notice the way they "coo." What is referred to as the "long-coo" is given in early spring and continues throughout the summer. Its sad, plaintive quality accounts for the bird's common name. Not *morning* but *mourning* dove. It certainly does sound as if it is in a perpetual state of mourning. In the book of Isaiah, after King Hezekiah had been sick and was recovering from his illness, he said, "I moan like a dove" (Isa 38:14).

[1] Donald Stokes, *A Guide to Bird Behavior Volume 2*, (Boston: Little, Brown and Company, 1983), 55-57.

In another place, Isaiah speaks for the people of Israel, "like doves we moan mournfully" (Isa 59:11). From time to time, many of us echo the mournful sound of the dove. We moan as we mourn the experiences of loss which are so much a part of life. (Remember what I noted about the doves witnessing the crucifixion.)

I'd probably be a mourning dove if I weren't a human being. In the book of Hosea, the prophet said that his nation had "become like a dove, silly and without sense" (Hos 7:11). That's probably the impression most of us have of the mourning dove. They are so slow when avoiding a car on the road they seem mentally challenged. Jesus used them as a metaphor for purity. He told the disciples to be "wise as serpents and innocent as doves" (Mt 10:16). The dove, for me, has always given the impression of being rather gentle, passive, harmless. It's no wonder it has become the symbol of peace.

The gospel writers also chose to use the dove as the symbol for the Holy Spirit. It's one of the few things that they agree on. Luke said that when Jesus was baptized by John, as he was praying, "the heaven was opened, and the Holy Spirit descended upon him in bodily form like a dove" (Lk 3:21-22). Matthew says it even alighted on him.

I read somewhere that in the medieval church, heavenly scenes would be painted on the great domed and vaulted ceilings of the cathedrals. They would often disguise small trap doors in the ceiling opening to the rooftop. During the Pentecost worship service, servants would climb up on the roof. At the appropriate moment during the liturgy, they would release live doves through these holes. From out of the painted skies and clouds on the cathedral ceiling, swooping, diving symbols of the Holy Spirit would descend toward the people below. They called those openings to the sky "Holy Spirit holes." Most churches I know need a *Holy Spirit Hole!* Maybe more of us need a Holy Spirit Hole in our soul.

I once heard of a pastor who went into the sanctuary of his church as it was being constructed, and he noticed the huge limestone altar had been installed upside down. He knew that because he noticed the dove etched into the stone was ascending, not descending. It was not coming to rest upon the church but flying away from it. There are probably times in our lives when we feel like that. It seems like God is leaving us, not on the way to be with us.

For me, the real significance of the dove in the Bible is found in the story of Noah and the ark. The story ought to be familiar to us. All life and living things were gone, except Noah and his family and a menagerie of animals crammed together in the ark. He could see nothing but water. No vision, no hope, no solution. They had been on that smelly, cramped ark for one hundred fifty days. Noah probably felt God had forgotten about him. In fact, the first verse of the eighth chapter of Genesis begins, "But God remembered Noah and all the wild animals and all the domestic animals that were with him in the ark." God began to act. God made a wind blow over the earth, and the waters receded. The rain subsided. The waters gradually disappeared from the earth. The ark came to rest on Mount Ararat. Eventually, they could see the tops of the mountains.

Noah began to hope. He opened the window of the ark and sent out a raven. The raven is listed in Leviticus as one of the unclean birds, which meant the Jewish people were forbidden to eat it. We are told “it went to and fro until the waters were dried up from the earth" (Gen 8:7). It probably fed upon the carcasses that were left from the flood.

After the raven, Noah sent out a dove. The dove needed life to survive, a living tree to perch on, fruit growing from the earth to eat. When he first sent out the dove, it came right back, having found no place to set its foot. Noah waited another week and again sent out the dove. It came back to him that night, and "there in its beak was a freshly plucked olive leaf; so Noah knew that the waters had subsided from the earth" (Gen 8:11). He couldn’t see the land, but he knew it was there. He waited seven more days and when he again sent out the dove, it did not return to him. It had found dry ground. What Noah did was much like our praying. We send "up" our prayers like he sent out the dove. Sometimes we just have to wait.

One of the most powerful images of the entire Bible is surely that dove flying back to the ark with an olive leaf in its beak! That image has long been a profound symbol of peace. (Some interpret that to mean God had stopped warring against humanity.) Both the olive branch and the dove are symbols of the promise of better times to come. It’s probably no coincidence that the dove brought back a branch of an olive tree. The Bible would refer to the olive tree and its oil as an extremely vital plant to the people. Despite the wars that have ravaged the land of the Bible through the ages, olive trees have persevered. Even when rampaging armies cut down orchards, the trees returned, sprouting up from their tenacious roots, often producing several trees where one grew before. As Robert Young has written, "Noah knew, from just a sprig, there must be solid ground somewhere! Not much. But it doesn't take much—just a sprig of hope."[2]

I read not long ago that there are people who will bring their doves to funerals and cemeteries to release them. Even weddings. They are said to represent the spirits of the departed.

We simply cannot survive without hope. Some hopeful signs, some glimmer of hope. Without hope, we would just give up. There is an old story told about a town in Maine that was to be flooded as part of a large lake for which a dam was being built. In the months before it was to be flooded, all improvements and repairs in the whole town were stopped. What was the use of painting a house if it were to be covered with water in six months? Why repair anything when the whole village was to be wiped out? Week by week, the whole town became more and more bedraggled. It was said by one citizen of the town, "Where there is no faith in the future, there is no power in the present." It has been said that hope is "hearing the melody of the future and dancing to that melody in the here and now."

The flood may be a parable for us. We can often feel overwhelmed, in over our heads, sinking, swamped. We may look around for some evidence of solid ground. Sometimes just a sprig of hope will do it for us. Henri Nouwen wrote that hope is like discovering land in the midst of a gale at sea. We need something solid, secure, sure; something that endures, that lasts, that is certain, in the midst of so much turmoil in life. It's hope that moves us to take the next step because we believe tomorrow will be better. It's what we feel when we begin a new job, a new friendship, or visit a new church. It's what keeps us taking our medicine and keeping our doctor's appointments. "Is there any hope?" is what we are always asking. That's because, as someone put it, "Hope is the essential ingredient of life. Every great religion, every political movement has offered hope." It may well be the greatest need we have.

G. K. Chesterton said that "Hope means hoping when things are hopeless, or it is no virtue at all...As long as matters are really hopeful, hope is mere flattery or platitude; it is only when everything is hopeless that hope begins to be a strength."

A number of years ago researchers performed an experiment to see the effect hope has on those undergoing hardship. Two sets of laboratory rats were placed in separate tubs of water. The researchers left one set in the

[2] Robert T. Young, *A Sprig of Hope: Sermons of Encouragement & Expectation*, (United States: Abingdon, 1980).

water and found that within an hour they had all drowned. The other rats were periodically lifted out of the water and then returned. When that happened, the second set of rats swam for over 24 hours. Why? Not because they were given a rest, but because they suddenly had hope. Those animals somehow hoped that if they could stay afloat just a little longer, someone would reach down and rescue them. If hope holds such power for rats, how much greater should its effect be on us.

Hope is hanging on to the *better* end, not just bitter end. It's knowing that we can accept the losses in life with the assurance that there may be something better. We still have hope, no matter what happens to us. Let me share a couple very moving illustrations of the power of hope. (I have permission to use them from the persons involved.) A couple years ago at Christmas I received a letter from a good friend of mine, who was the news anchor on one of our local stations. She and her husband had moved to Cincinnati where she continued in television news. They had one son whom I had been privileged to hold very soon after his birth. In her Christmas card she told me she was at her parents' home recovering after suffering a third loss of a baby. She wrote, "Each loss takes us to the brink, but it's as if God gives us the strength to fight our way back each time…We have such faith and trust that this will work out for good some day!" The next September I received a letter from her in which she said that three renowned doctors had told them to give up--that another child was just not meant to be. But she and her husband had decided not to give up. Then she wrote this: "Bill, tonight, I sit in a hospital bed where just 24 hours ago I gave birth to the most beautiful little girl! By the way, we named her Grace."

I received a letter from another member of the church I was serving.

> "One of the first few sermons we heard you preach was on hope. I wanted you to know how profoundly that sermon affected me. My husband and I had been trying for almost two years to have another child… You specifically mentioned couples trying to have children and couldn't, to always remember they had hope. I never forgot that sermon. I remained hopeful during two miscarriages and a year and a half of failed fertility treatments. I'm happy to say we were blessed with another pregnancy and are expecting a baby very soon. I wanted to thank you for reminding me that I always can hope."

May those testimonies to the power of faith and trust be sprigs of hope for you, regardless of your situation. Don't play the postlude when you should be playing the prelude. It's like the difference between a fellow saying "I lost my job" and "I'm in between jobs." Sometimes an ending is really a new beginning.

Questions for Contemplating and Conversing

1. When have you felt the most hopeless in your life?
2. What gives you hope?
3. What would you say to a friend who is feeling hopeless to give them at least a glimpse of hope?
4. What is the difference between hope and faith?
5. Why do you think the dove became a symbol of the Holy Spirit? A symbol of peace?
6. What does a dove symbolize for you?
7. What is the main lesson you learned from this chapter?

5. Mockingbirds

Read Matthew 5 and 6; Ephesians 5

You are an A+ student of the scriptures if you know mockingbirds aren't mentioned in the Bible. I am not sure if they were among the 350 species of birds found in Palestine in Jesus' day, but they are fairly common where I live. Most of us have at least heard them. I don't know the scientific name for many birds, but the one for the Mockingbird is pretty interesting: *Mimus polyglottos.* I can't translate the Latin literally, but it sounds like "many-tongued impersonator," doesn't it? We know the mockingbird because its song is usually a continual stream of other birds' calls, each call usually repeated three or more times. (The catbird is another bird that frequently imitates other birds' calls, and I've even read starlings can do that.) I know of a bird-lover who used the mockingbird to teach his kids birdsong identification. They would lie on their lawn listening to their mockingbird sing, and after each little burst of song, they would call out the name of the species.

But the most prominent aspect of the mockingbird's behavior is territoriality. They have small, sharply defined and aggressively defended territories. They form them twice each year, once in spring for breeding and again in the fall to protect a winter food source. The territory is marked by the mockingbird's loud, imitative song. The spring territory is centered on the nest; the fall territory is centered on a source of food. In the spring, its defensive behavior is directed toward people, dogs, cats, snakes, large birds and other animals that are a threat to the nest. In the fall, the bird protects its food source from robins, starlings, and blue jays. And both times, the territory is defended against other mockingbirds, as well.

Food sources have a bearing on the size of the territory. Most territories of songbirds in America range from about half an acre or less, to several acres. Other needs filled by territorialism include the maintenance of the bond between a pair of birds, the reduction of interference, and the regulation of the density of a species in a favorable habitat.

One naturalist said we are as much territorial animals as is a mockingbird. If you don't believe in our own territorial instinct, you haven't read anything about the Middle East, Eastern Europe, or Africa. Or wondered about those who live in gated communities or secure subdivisions. There is also that territorial spirit of "Not in my backyard." And all the conflicts over annexation and zoning. We go to war to "protect our nation's interests and security," which is another way of saying we protect our territory.

Sometimes our lives are reduced to nothing more than just protecting our territory, which can be little more than "nest" and "food sources." Our lives can be reduced to going from home to store and back again. Or to the mailbox to return something we had ordered on-line. We can narrowly define our area of concern and interest. It may be no larger than the size of our country club or favorite golf course. Or worse, about the size of the screen of our cell phone! In her poem, "Renascence," Edna St. Vincent Millay wrote,

> The world stands out on either side
> No wider than the heart is wide;
> Above the world is stretched the sky, --
> No higher than the soul is high.[1]

Some of us have a pretty small world, because our hearts and souls are just too small. That's something we may learn from watching birds, especially the mockingbird. We can become too "territorial."

What I really want you to consider, though, is how birds communicate. We may have thought that birds sing to greet the spring or the sun, or to proclaim their joy in just being alive, but mostly what they are communicating is "Stay out of my neighborhood!" to enemies, and "I am

[1] Edna St. Vincent Millay, "Renascence," *Renascence and Other Poems*, (New York: Harper, 1917).

attractive" and "Come hither!" to potential mates. Their songs are mostly an announcement of status and tough talk to rivals. Singing becomes more frequent and more aggressive when another male is within hearing. But the songs are also used to strengthen the bond between a pair of birds during the short nesting season. They are also associated with group movements and flocking, finding food, warning of enemies, and parent-young relationships. Some birds have evening flight songs that are sung only for the female they are courting and at no other time of the year. Someone has said we understand why birds sing, but we don't know why they sing so *beautifully*.

Most of us know at least a few birds by their calls or songs. You can't miss the owl, the whip-poor-will or the bobwhite quail. I don't know if you ever heard the peewee (yes, that is a bird), but it's known by the way it repeats its name over and over again. You probably know the difference between the songs of a song sparrow and a robin. And once I even heard a hummingbird (they don't really hum because they forgot the words to the song, but they don't sing either.) I understand the red-eyed vireo is called the "preacher bird" because of the monotonous repetition of its phrases. One vireo was reported to have repeated his refrain over 22,000 times between dawn and dark. The most modestly colored birds are among the most gifted singers. It's their only advertisement, I guess.

It's fascinating to listen to a mockingbird from some distance and realize you are not listening to the bird being imitated. I've been fooled often. They have quite a repertoire. And their songs always sound quite joyful—even in the middle of the night or after he has lost his mate.

Mockingbirds are a part of a group of birds that are called *continuous singers*. They can imitate 30 other species. In California, they will even imitate tree frogs.

Birds have been called "the most instinctively musical of all creatures." I can't help but think sometimes songs of birds are hymns of joy. I'd like to think so. Observers have suggested that the songs of birds possess all the basic elements of music: rhythm, tones, harmony and melody. I also read that birds probably find fulfillment in singing and the more demanding the song, the higher the degree of fulfillment it finds.

I don't want to push this too far, but one cannot help but be uplifted when listening to a bird sing at dawn or twilight. It may even make us want to join in. And that is what we are to do. St. Augustine said "A hymn is the praise of God by singing." A hymn is a song embodying the praise of God. Singing is probably the most genuinely popular element in

Christian worship. In a sense, great hymns "put words in our mouths," and the greatest ones cause us to think, "That's what I wanted to say." Likewise, the Psalms offer us expressions of what we are thinking and feeling. Paul wrote to the Ephesians that we are to be filled with the Spirit, "as you sing psalms and hymns and spiritual songs among yourselves, singing and making melody to the Lord in your hearts, giving thanks to God the Father at all times and for everything in the name of our Lord Jesus Christ" (Eph 5:19-20).

Maybe we can learn to sing and praise God from listening to the birds, especially to the mockingbird. After all, we use music composed by someone else to give voice to our own feelings of joy.

When I originally began to think about what we might learn when we look at and listen to the mockingbird, I thought it might serve to remind us that too often we simply mimic, imitate, echo, conform to, and copy what others are doing. The mockingbird has no other song except a borrowed one. If we only sing the songs that others do, we fail to find what is often called "our own voice." In a book on preaching I read some time ago, the authors said the key to effective preaching is all about finding our own voice, expressing ourselves, making ourselves known. The authors say we have to learn to value our own thoughts, emotions, and experiences when we preach. One teacher of preaching says "every preacher has a 'voice'—a distinctive pattern of substance and expression that could be traced from sermon to sermon." There is always that danger that we end up as echoes of all the other voices we hear.

Not long ago I happened to see the title of a book, *The Influence of Oscar Wilde on W.B. Yeats: "An Echo of Someone Else's Music."* The playwright had an enormous influence on the younger poet. But there is a difference between influence and imitation. We should never settle for being nothing more than an echo.

Most of us probably start by imitation: by listening to and learning from those who are successful in our field. We may even try to be just like them. But the time comes when we realize we have to express ourselves in our own voice and with our own sound, and that no one is better or worse than anyone else. We are just different, that's all.

I think the same is true regardless of who we are or what our profession is. We must be true to ourselves. That's why Jesus said, "Be perfect, therefore, as your heavenly Father is perfect" (Mt 5:48) which is incorrectly translated, some scholars suggest. What he meant was, "Be complete" or "Be all you were meant to be." Simply, "Be you." I've heard it said that almost all frustration and anxiety come from a refusal to be what one is, the result of playing a part other than the one you have been given.

Indeed, you are the world's "one and only." The world doesn't need more "carbon copies" of a few. Too many of us constantly compare ourselves to others, usually envying some gift they have. (I confess I coveted the melodious voice of some of my fellow preachers.)

Martin Buber told an old story of the Hasidic Rabbi Zusya. On his deathbed he cried uncontrollably, so much that one of his students asked him, "Rabbi, why do you weep?" Zusya answered, "I don't worry that God will ask me, 'Zusya, why were you not more like Abraham, or Moses?' But what will I say when God asks me, 'Zusya, why were you not more like Zusya?'"[2]

All my life I wanted to be a writer. As a result, I've read many books on writing. Most all of them deal with "the writer's voice." A literary agent defines it: "Your writer's voice is the expression of YOU on the page." It has been said that you can identify the author by merely reading a selection of their work. Mary Karr, in her book *The Art of Memoir,* writes, "Each voice is cleverly fashioned to highlight a writer's individual talent or way of viewing the world."[3]

It has been estimated that there are between 250,00 and 400,000 Elvis impersonators in the world today. Though some of them are really good, the one thing they have in common is that they most likely don't have his talent. Some of us become really good at imitation, ending up as nothing more than genuine reproductions. We may become more like those we imitate than they are. True story: Years ago, there was a Charlie Chaplin look-alike contest held in Monte Carlo. Some of Charlie's best friends were there to do the judging. They were unaware that Charlie himself had entered the contest. He ended up in third place!

Sometimes we can become so very effective in being someone else, we have no idea who we are. I can remember when actor Peter Sellers died, it was reported that he had once said he had played so many parts, he never discovered who he was. You don't have to be a professional impersonator or actor to come to that same realization. God has need of the unique gifts and strengths each one of us has to offer to this place and time. The only person God wants you to be like is you. God wants you to be who you are. How ridiculous for us to grow into God's image in someone else.

[2] *Tales of the Hassidim: The Early Masters*, (New York: Shocken Books, 1968), 141.
[3] Mary Karr, *The Art of Memoir*, (New York: Harper Collins, 2015), 35.

Anglican Bishop Rowan Williams says that "it is God's desire for us to be the persons we are." Williams says, "The Holy Spirit calls us to be more, not less, ourselves—teaching Peter to be more Peter, John to be more John..."[4] God wants you to be more of who you really are.

It's not easy to do that. We live in a society that seems to put a premium on blending in, not standing out. Education often consists of our "regurgitating" what we are taught and told. Doing it the same as everyone else. Something I read years ago made a lasting impression on me. In his book, *To A Dancing God*, Sam Keen recalled being in Mrs. Jones' first-grade class. He said that one long afternoon he sat practicing his penmanship exercises, "listening to Mrs. Jones' monotone." "'Make your *i's* come all the way up to the middle line. And don't forget to make your *o's* nice and round. Circle, circle, circle. Period. Now repeat.'" He said he settled in to wait for the resurrection, the 3:00 o'clock bell, and then some movement in a tree outside the window caught his eye. In the light of the springtime world, he saw a summer warbler building a nest. He began to dream of the time he would become a great ornithologist, and forgot his i's and o's until Mrs. Jones came up behind him and asked why three lines in his penmanship book were empty. So, he realized no serendipitous warbler could provide him an excuse for the neglect of his serious educational duties, and he bit his tongue, cherished his wonder in silence, and stayed in after school to make up his lessons.

Keen said that schooling became a habit for him and he remained in the classroom for twenty-five years and five degrees with little enthusiasm. But, he said, "I learned little about the organization, appreciation, management, and care of that unique piece of human real estate which bears the legal name Sam Keen." He said when he finally left the classroom, he could dot his i's and make his o's round, "But the warbler was gone...I had gotten an education but lost an identity."[5] I especially like the phrase "that unique piece of human real estate which bears the legal name Sam Keen." Each of us is a unique piece of real estate. That's our real "territory" and we have to protect it from those who would intrude and rob us of our identity.

I am told that when an Eskimo carver holds a raw fragment of ivory in his hand, he turns it gently this way and that, whispering to it, "Who are

[4] Rowan Williams, *A Ray of Darkness*, (United State: Cowley Publication, 1995), 166.
[5] Sam Keen, *To A Dancing God: Education for Serendipity*, (San Francisco: Harper and Row, 1970), 38-39.

you? Who hides in you?" I suspect that we would find within each of us the person we'd like to be and were created to be.

Questions for Contemplating and Conversing

1. Have there been times you have tried to be someone other than yourself? What came of that?
2. What do you envy about other persons?
3. What do you think about Oscar Wilder's quote: "Imitation is the sincerest form of flattery that mediocrity can pay to greatness"?
4. What makes you unique, one-of-a-kind?
5. Are you always the "real you"? Why or why not?
6. What does it mean to be *genuine*?
7. In what ways was Jesus unique, one-of-a-kind, and genuine?
8. What is the main lesson you learned from this chapter?

6. Ostriches

Read Job 39:13-18

When I told a member of my church I wanted to preach a series of sermons on "The Birds of the Air," based on Jesus's admonition to look at them, and to focus on ostriches in one of them, he told me that "ostriches don't fly and shouldn't be called a bird of the air."

It's true that an ostrich isn't a bird that you are ever going to look at in the air, since they can't fly, and the only place most of us will ever see them is in a zoo. But they were common in biblical times. They were not held in very high regard. They inhabited the wasted areas. Isaiah declared that after God had destroyed God's earthly enemies, the land would be good for nothing but ravens, jackals, hyenas, hedgehogs and *ostriches* (Isa 34:11-14). In the book of Lamentations, it says that people had become cruel, "like the ostriches in the wilderness" (Lam 4:3). You know that because of his suffering and lot in life, Job felt ostracized. In one place he complained, "I am a brother of jackals, and a companion of ostriches" (Job 30:29). Later in the book, when Job and God are talking, God compares Job to the stupid ostrich, whom God had made to "forget wisdom, and given it no share in understanding (Job 39:17). I don't know how stupid they really are, but they sure do look stupid, don't they? Kind of like they were designed by a committee. There is an Arabic saying: "more stupid than an ostrich."

An ostrich is the largest living bird, now found mainly in Africa. They reach a height of nearly eight feet, and almost half of their height is neck.

They weigh more than 300 pounds. Their eggs weigh up to three pounds. They live in flocks. They can live 50 years. They rely on their strong legs to escape their enemies, mostly humans and the larger carnivores. A frightened ostrich can achieve a speed of 40 miles an hour. And if cornered it can deliver dangerous kicks. They are uniquely two-toed, with the main toe developed almost as a hoof. Before it gets to that, to escape detection, they lie on the ground with neck outstretched, a habit that may have given rise to the legend that the ostrich buries its head in the sand when danger threatens.

Today there are ostrich farms, where they are raised for their plumage and for their meat. There is even an American Ostrich Association. There may be something we can learn from looking at them. It occurred to me that there are three defense mechanisms utilized by the ostrich when facing danger: Fight, flight and "out of sight." They can fight, and often inflict serious injury with their strong, muscular legs. They can flee, running on the ground at incredible speeds. They "bury their heads in the sand," as if to avoid dealing with the threat and fool themselves into thinking they are safe. Not too dissimilar from how you and I react to threatening situations and deal with problems, is it? We "out-of-sight" them—deny them. We are frightened and run from them, or we face them and fight them. Let's talk about those responses to trouble.

One of the most common responses to problems of any sort is to deny them. Individuals do that; so do families, and entire groups can be in a state of denial. We can keep telling ourselves, for example, that there are no drug problems in our city or in our schools, that there is no racism in our congregation or community. We "bury our heads in the sand," oblivious to what's going on around us. There's a proverb that says, "There is none so blind as he who will not see." We ignore things. We use denial as a coping mechanism. You are aware that Dr. Elizabeth Kubler-Ross' first stage in dealing with death and dying is denial. She said the first reaction to the awareness of a terminal illness is usually, "No, not me, it cannot be true." We may even fool ourselves into thinking that we can hide from trouble. My dad used to talk about how some people wish they had an "unlisted life" when trouble comes looking for them. When Jesus announced to the disciples that he would suffer and be put to death on a cross, Peter rebukes him, "God forbid it, Lord! This must never happen to you." A lot of people echo that: "It can't happen to me!"

Scott Goodyear, racecar driver, said that he doesn't pay attention to where an accident happened. "You don't watch the films of it on television. You don't deal with it. You pretend it never happened." I read that throughout the history of the Indianapolis Motor Speedway, a driver has never been pronounced dead at the racetrack. The Museum has no memorial to the 40 drivers who have lost their lives there. As soon as the track closes the day of an accident, a crew heads out to paint over the spot where the car hit the wall. I think Jesus said something about "whitewashing" the ugly side of life. And the captain of the Titanic refused to believe the ship was in trouble until water was ankle deep in the mailroom.

Many people I know try to cover the harsh realities of life with a smile. They try to hide their anger and their anxiety. I know of one minister who said he figured some of television preachers who promote a kind of faith that refuses to acknowledge reality, actually believe in a "perpetually grinning Jesus, even on the Cross." One day, in 1942, a man named Felix Powell sat down at a piano to play an old tune. He had written it himself. It had been tremendously popular in both World Wars. He began singing: "So pack up your troubles in your old kit bag, and smile, smile, smile." When Felix Powell finished his song, he walked into his bedroom, took out a revolver, put it to his head, and shot himself. He could write a song about not worrying, but he was unable to overcome his worries himself.

A psychologist is quoted as saying, "Most of our unhappiness and emotional struggles are caused by the lies we tell ourselves; until we identify our lies and replace them with the truth, emotional well-being is impossible." Refusal to face the pain that accompanies life is not healthy. It can be detrimental to our physical, emotional, and spiritual well-being. When we try to deny how tough life can be, we may end up keeping God at a distance, never allowing God to give us the help God promised.

We are equally good at fleeing. Like the ostrich, we have mastered the flight pattern of response. We all know how to run away from terrifying or overwhelming situations. There are a number of ways we try to escape. We refuse to accept responsibility. We blame. We make ourselves out to be victims. We can run by constantly moving, taking another job, traveling, looking for a new start somewhere else, wanting a change of scenery. A young college student was talking about his grades in school and said, "They're not good—not good at all. But I'm going to transfer to another school next year." The problem is, it's a never-ending journey. As Br'er Fox said to Peter Rabbit: "You can't run away from trouble. There ain't no place that far!"

Do you remember the Broadway musical from several years back, "Stop the World--I Want to Get Off"? Have you felt that way? I understand there was a place in a police station in one city called the "Give Up Room." When the detectives and police officers got weary of chasing criminals and were feeling scared of going out into dangerous streets, they'd go to that room to relax, drink coffee--and wait for the criminal to come in and give himself up—which, of course, hardly ever happened. Maybe we'd all like a "give up room" where we can just sit and wait for things to work out for us. We are tempted to get away, give up.

Even though ostriches can't do it, one of the escape mechanisms of other birds is actual *flight*. What most of us want are wings, so that we can fly away. That reminds me of the Psalm,

My heart is in anguish within me,
the terrors of death have fallen upon me.
Fear and trembling come upon me,
And horror overwhelms me,
And I say, "O that I had wings like a dove!
I would fly away and be at rest;
Truly, I would flee far away;
I would lodge in the wilderness;
I would hurry to find a shelter for myself
From the raging wind and tempest." (Ps 55:4-8)

It's no coincidence that the name Jonah means "dove." Certainly, he was the prime example of someone who wanted to escape, fly away, and escape responsibility. There are times in our lives when we just want to fly away, flee, and get away from things as they are. We have all sorts of wings: drugs, alcohol, sleep, suicide—all providing a flight from reality. We are aware of any number of people who are running away. They have a pathological desire to escape from the difficulties, the drudgeries, and the realities of life. They are always looking for the exit. If they don't love it, they leave it. The land of dreams is close at hand, so they can escape into it at any moment, to get away from painful reality. Other people flee into the past, reliving the good old days. We can also flee into our work and even into religion.

A British officer in India, warned that he was drinking too heavily, lifted his glass and said, "My friend, this is the swiftest road out of India." The quickest way out of most anything is alcohol. We take a lot of other dangerous roads to escape: make-believe, fantasy, rationalization, evading reality. You don't have to read the Bible farther than the third chapter of Genesis until you meet up with someone who tries to run away from responsibility. Adam and Eve hid away from the presence of God among the trees. God called out to Adam, "Where are you?" Adam replied that he heard God in the garden, became afraid, and "I hid myself" (Gen 3:9-10). After killing an Egyptian, Moses fled from Pharaoh. Jacob fled from his brother Esau. David fled from Saul. In the New Testament, after Jesus was arrested, the disciples deserted him and fled.

Elijah was forced to flee for his life to escape the ire of Queen Jezebel. He was burned-out after the confrontation with the prophets of Baal on Mt. Carmel. He fled to Mount Horeb, where Moses had been given the law. He thought maybe he could find strength and healing to work against his profound discouragement in the place where Israel found its identity. He secured shelter in a cave and waited, hoping to find God, who seemed so painfully absent. You'll remember God came to him, not in the earthquake or the fire, but in a still small voice. Elijah told God, in self-pity and bitterness, "Everyone else has forsaken you and I alone am left." God told him he was not the only one who had remained faithful. And then he told Elijah to finish his job. "Go, return upon thy way to the wilderness of Damascus, and there you shall do a number of things, among which is the anointing of your successor. Go, for there are still things for you to do, and you cannot do them here" (my paraphrase of I Kings 19:9-18).

Whenever someone faced with a difficulty or problem in the Bible sought help from God, there was always the command to "go back and face it." God offers no escape from the realities of life, only a means of facing it confidently. That leads me to my third point.

We can face our troubles, our fears, and our problems. Fight them. Stand up to them. Face them. Look our fears and failures in the eye. When we are frightened, adrenaline hits the bloodstream and depending on our genetic predisposition, we react with either a fight-fear or flight-fear. We either lash out or retreat. Gus D'Amato, the renowned trainer of boxing champions, revealed great wisdom when he observed, "Heroes and cowards feel exactly the same fear; heroes just react differently."

When Nehemiah tried to rebuild the walls of Jerusalem, his enemies did everything they could to prevent it. They laughed it off, "What are these feeble Jews doing? Will they revive the stones out of the heaps of rubbish? That stone wall they are building—any fox going up on it would break it down!" But Nehemiah was oblivious to their taunts. Finally, they had to threaten him. That's when Nehemiah spoke those stirring words, "Should a man like me run away?" (Neh 4-6).

We never accomplish anything by running away from our problems, or seeking to escape from them. We need to face them head on. The worst fear is the fear of the unknown. That's why it's best to look at life squarely enough so that you know what it is that is troubling you.

The story is told of an old cowboy on a Western ranch. A minister went out to comfort him in his dying days. Sitting beside the bunk, the minister tried to divert the old man's thoughts away from his dying by getting him to talk about his life. "Tell me," the minister said, "what important truth that you learned from your experiences on the plains stands out in your memory at this time?" After a few moments of silence, the cowboy replied, "Well, sir, the Hereford cow has taught me one of life's most important lessons, I reckon. We used to breed cattle for a living, but the severe winter storms used to take an awful toll. Again and again after a severe storm, we would find most of the cattle piled up against the fences dead. These cattle would turn their backs to the icy winter blasts and slowly drift downward for twenty miles until the fences stopped them. There they piled up and died. But the Herefords were different. They would head straight into the wind and slowly work up the other way until they came to our upper boundary fence where they stood facing into the storm. We always found them alive and well. That's the greatest lesson I ever learned. The Herefords face the storm."

Eleanor Roosevelt was an extraordinary woman who knew courage. She once said, "You gain strength, courage, and confidence by every experience when you must stop and look fear in the face. You must do the thing you think you cannot do."[1] Emerson said, "Do the thing you fear and the death of fear is certain." Mark Twain said, "Courage is resistance to fear, mastery of fear, not absence of fear." General George Patton was praised profusely for his courage in World War II. But he admitted, "I am not a brave man. The truth of the matter is I am usually a coward at heart. I have never been in the sound of gunshot or sight of battle in my whole life that I was not afraid. I constantly have sweat on my palms and a lump in my throat." The difference was, he chose not to run.

Max Lucado has pointed out that one of the most feared thieves in the Old West was Black Bart. He terrorized the Wells Fargo stage line for

[1] Eleanor Roosevelt, *You Learn by Living: Eleven Keys for a More Fulfilled Life*, (New York: Harper Perennial, 2011).

years. His name became synonymous with the danger of the frontier. During his reign of terror between 1875 and 1883, he is credited with robbing twenty-nine different stagecoach crews. He did it without ever firing a shot. His weapon was his reputation. He wore a hood over his face. No victim ever saw him. No sheriff could ever track his trail. He could paralyze the bravest man by just appearing on the scene.

As it turns out, Black Bart wasn't anything to be afraid of. When they finally got his hood off, they only found a mild-mannered druggist from Decatur, Illinois, who was so afraid of horses that he rode to and from his robberies in a buggy. He was Charles E. Boles—the bandit who never once fired a shot because he never once loaded a gun.[2]

I mentioned how Jacob fled from his brother Esau. Esau had threatened to kill him, and probably had every right to do so. Jacob had stolen his birthright from him. Twenty years later, Jacob decides to return home. He learns that Esau is coming toward him with four hundred men. Jacob is afraid and distressed, quite obviously, and so he divides his belongings into two, so that half of his possessions might be safe. He prays, "[1]Deliver me, please, from the hand of my brother, from the hand of Esau, for I am afraid of him; he may come and kill us all, the mothers with the children" (Gen 32:11). When he gets closer to Esau, he is so terrified he even arranges for his family to go as a shield in front of him. Then comes the surprise of the story: "But Esau ran to meet him, and embraced him, and fell on his neck and kissed him, and they wept." Esau forgives him (33:4).

I suspect we can all remember when we had a falling-out with a friend, and that bitter edge of life grew worse and worse until we met him one day face-to-face and acknowledged the situation and then discovered there was some ground for reconciliation. It just may be that if we were to quit hiding or running from whatever it is that frightens and frustrates us in life, we would discover that it is far less intimidating than we feared. We will also discover how God is always there to help us.

Questions for Contemplating and Conversing

1. How do you handle bad news? Face it or try to ignore it?
2. Have you been successful in avoiding it and forgetting it?
3. Why do you think it is better in the long run to face a difficulty?
4. Are many of your fears *unfounded*?

[2] Max Lucado, *The Applause of Heaven*, (Dallas: Word, 1990), 77-78.

5. When have you *run the other way?*
6. What is the main lesson you learned from this chapter?

7. Vultures and Hummingbirds

Read Philippians 4:4-9

I want us to look at a couple of very different birds of the air to see what we might learn from them. I've known far more vulture and hummingbird people than I have eagles or mourning doves.

Vultures (or buzzards as I grew up calling them) are probably the ugliest birds God created. They have those featherless heads. And the behavior is no better. They are scavengers. They eat carrion, road kill, and garbage. You've probably seen them soaring in wide circles looking for meat in various stages of putrefaction. They are hard to miss, with a wingspan of up to nine feet.

Hummingbirds, on the other hand, are probably the most delightful visitors to our yards. John James Audubon called them "Glittering fragments of the rainbow." A ruby-throated hummingbird weighs only a tenth of an ounce and measures less than four inches in length. They winter in Mexico and Central America. They migrate back North, flying nonstop across the Gulf of Mexico—a distance of 600 miles--on the fat they store beforehand, just as the flowers they feed on are coming into bloom. They can fly in any direction, including backward; they can hover, shift sideways, and also fly straight up or down. They beat their wings up to 55 times a second and can achieve speeds of around 50 mph. They consume 50% of their weight in sugar each day. They are especially attracted to nectar-rich, red tubular flowers.[1] An average blossom provides about enough energy for the hummingbird to fly for about 11 seconds.

Vultures spend their lives looking for rotting stuff. Hummingbirds look for what is sweet and good. Steve Goodier described the differences between them in this way:

> Both the hummingbird and the vulture fly over our nation's deserts. All vultures see is rotting meat, because that is what they look for. They thrive on that diet. But hummingbirds ignore the smelly flesh of dead animals. Instead, they look for the colorful blossoms of desert plants. The vultures live on what was. They live on the past. They fill themselves with what is dead and gone. But hummingbirds live on what is. They seek new life. They fill themselves with freshness and life. Each bird finds what it is looking for. We all do.[2]

"Each bird finds what it is looking for. We all do." Most all of us really do find what we're looking for in life, don't we? That's true of both situations and other people. A traveler nearing a city asked a man, seated by the wayside, "What are the people like in this city?" The man replied, "How were the people where you came from?" "A terrible lot," the traveler responded, "Mean, untrustworthy, detestable in all respects." "Ah," said the man, "you will find them the same in the city ahead." Scarcely was the first traveler gone when another man stopped and also inquired about the people in the city up ahead. Again, the old man asked about the people in the place the traveler had left. "They were fine people; honest, industrious, and generous to a fault. I was sorry to leave," declared the second traveler. Responded the wise man, "So you will find them in the city ahead."

Charles Swindoll was right: "The longer I live, the more I realize the impact of attitude on life…The remarkable thing is we have a choice every day regarding the attitude we will embrace for that day…I am convinced that life is 10 percent what happens to me and 90 percent how I react to it…We are in charge of our attitudes!"[3]

[1] Donald and Lillian Stokes, *A Guide to Bird Behavior Volume 3*, 255-265.
[2] Steve Goodier, Quote Magazine, in Reader's Digest, May, 1990.
[3] Charles R. Swindoll, Quotes, (Author of *The Grace Awakening*), https://www.goodreads.com.

I once heard of a woman's epitaph that said, "Ever she sought the good and ever she found it." What a wonderful testimonial. If you go through life seeking the bad, you won't be disappointed. If you go through life seeking the good, you won't be disappointed. You'll always find what you are looking for. There's an old Jewish proverb that says, "We do not see things as they are but as we are."

If you don't believe that, how else can you explain the fact that people go through the same experience with quite different reactions? A part of it, of course, is due to the difference in our needs, but I think it's due in large part to what we expect and what we are looking for. There's a good way to tell the difference between people with positive attitudes and those with negative attitudes. It's like what the Israelite army said when they encountered Goliath: "He's so big we'll never kill him!" David reframed the question and changed the perspective: "He's so big I can't miss him!" Which would you have said?

I'm sure you've known your share of "vultures." I have. They are the ones who seem determined to find something wrong about everything and everybody. I don't know enough psychology to understand what's behind that kind of negative attitude. But I remember a story of the sailor who drank too much and fell asleep at his table in the bar. His buddies smeared a bit of strong-smelling cheese dip on his mustache, and that made him wake up and look around. He sniffed and then walked outside, sniffed again, and came back in. He walked out and back in one more time and finally sat down in his chair. "It's no use," he said to a friend, "the whole world stinks!" I guess there are just some people who have something in them that makes them feel the whole world stinks.

It's like the widow who had two sons on whom she relied for financial support. One son sold umbrellas. The other son sold fans. The first thing the mother did every morning was look out to see if the sun was shining or if it looked like rain. If it were raining, she'd get depressed because without the sun's heat, nobody was likely to buy a fan. If the sun was shining, she'd get depressed because nobody was going to buy an umbrella from her other son. Now, of course, she could have looked at it in the totally opposite way and realize she couldn't lose either way, but she didn't.

That's like the difference between beginning the day with a "Good Lord, morning!" and "Good morning, Lord!" Choosing our attitude and our expectations is like putting on glasses in the morning. If we put on glasses with clean lenses, then things will look pretty good to us. If we put on glasses with dirty lenses, then things will only look rather messy. In Norman Vincent Peale's classic, *The Power of Positive Thinking,* he makes the point that "if you expect the worst you will get the worst, and if you expect the best you will get the best." He tells the story of the time a baseball team fell into a slump and lost seventeen of their next twenty games. The manager realized his players were thinking wrong. They didn't expect to get a hit; they didn't expect to win; they expected to be defeated. He asked each player to loan him his two best bats. He took the bats to a preacher who was reported to be a faith healer. When the manager returned, he told them the preacher had blessed the bats and that the bats now contained a power that could not be overcome. The players were astonished and delighted. The next day they got 37 base hits and scored 20 runs. They went on to win the championship that year. Years after that, players would pay large sums for one of those "blessed" bats.[4]

That's going to be true of any experience. You'll probably get what you're looking for. A British psychiatrist did an experiment to find out whether people who believe in the reality of the Monday blues are more likely to feel bad on Monday. He gave one group a report that said Monday blues are for real. He gave a second group a report that denied the existence of such a thing. The third group received nothing to read. You guessed it: the first group, those told that there really is something to the Monday blues, were more likely to rate Monday as the worst day in the week. He concluded that how people expect to feel affects how they do feel.

If you find yourself saying, "What's wrong?" more often than you say, "What's right?" you might be a vulture. If you are always looking for what's wrong in other people, rather than what's good about them, you may be a vulture. On the other hand, hummingbirds feed on the stuff Paul wrote about: "…whatever is true, whatever is honorable, whatever is just, whatever is pure, whatever is pleasing, whatever is commendable, if there is any excellence and if there is anything worthy of praise, think about these things" (Phil 4:8). Let me emphasize that: "If there is *anything* worthy of praise…"

We especially need to do that with other people. There are far too many vultures circling around us all the time, waiting to find what's bad about us. We need more hummingbirds looking for what's good. Laurie Beth Jones writes that Jesus "did not spend one minute on the demolition crew.

[4] Norman Vincent Peale, *The Power of Positive Thinking*, (New York: Prentice-Hall, 1952), 108.

He spent his energy on creation and restoration."[5] The expectations we have of others can greatly influence their feelings and behaviors. We can crush them with criticism, or we can encourage them to grow with our affirmation. Jesus certainly did that when he called the flaky Simon, "Peter," which means, "rock solid." Our words can have tremendous power for enabling and ennobling.

When we assume a negative attitude and reflect to others all the data about their weaknesses, we put them in touch with their faults and their behavior becomes worse. But, if we assume a positive attitude and concentrate on their strong aspects, we put them in contact with their good attributes and their behavior becomes better. In other words, we have the power to make them into either vultures or hummingbirds when it comes to how they feel about themselves.

In a famous study by a Harvard psychologist, it was discovered that by raising the teacher's expectations they could raise the children's performances as well, and that some children perform poorly in school simply because their teachers expect them to. Some of the teachers of children in a group of kindergarten through fifth-grade pupils were told that certain children had exceptional learning ability. That wasn't the case; they had been selected at random. But at the end of the school year, all the children whom the teachers thought had the most potential had actually scored far ahead of the others and had gained as many as 15 to 27 I. Q. points. The teachers described these children as happier, more curious, more affectionate than average, and as having a better chance of success in later life. The only change throughout the year was the change in attitudes of the teachers.

What a difference that could make in our homes. A couple married for fifteen years began having more than the usual number of disagreements. They wanted to make their marriage work and agreed on an idea the wife had. For one month they planned to drop a slip of paper in a "Fault" box. The boxes would provide a place to let the other know about daily irritations. The wife was diligent in her efforts. She put in criticisms like "leaving the jelly top off the jar," "wet towels on the shower floor," "dirty socks not in hamper," on and on until she had filled the jar. After dinner, at the end of the month, they exchanged boxes. The husband read all that he had done wrong. Then the wife opened her box and began reading. All the pieces were the same. The message on each slip was "I love you."

[5] Laurie Beth Jones, *Jesus, CEO, 25th Anniversary Edition*, (Paris: Hachette, 2021).

Obviously, he had been looking for, and finding, what was good. Sometimes it's all about what we are willing to overlook, not just what we look for.

Questions for Contemplating and Conversing

1. Are you generally a positive or negative person? Why do you say that?
2. Are you more comfortable being around positive or negative people? Why do you say that?
3. Do you look for the good in other persons? In situations and experiences?
4. How powerful is one's attitude?
5. How does the Christian faith make us more positive?
6. What is the main lesson you learned from this chapter?

8. Sparrows

Read Matthew 10:29-31

I suspect we all have our favorite birds. Maybe for you it's the Indiana state bird, the cardinal. It might be a goldfinch (or wild canary as I was taught to call them), the house wren, or a less-common bird, like the indigo bunting (which was my favorite bird when I was a child). My mother's favorite bird was the sparrow. The house sparrow. Your everyday, standard-brand sparrow. Mom liked them, she said, because they reminded her of "common people." She liked ordinary, down-to-earth, plain folks. Maybe it was because that's who we were.

Perhaps they were Jesus' favorite bird, too. We know the "common people heard him gladly," and flocked to him. He might have liked the sparrow for the same reason my mother did. He said that they had value in the eyes of God, even if they were not the favorite birds of many, if any, people back then or even now. I suspect Jesus selected the sparrow for his object lesson because sparrows were nearly worthless. Literally. They were sold in the marketplaces of Palestine as inexpensive food for the poor. Two for a penny. They were so cheap that if you bought four of them, you usually got one thrown in free. Jesus was saying that he couldn't think of anything more worthless than a sparrow. But in the eyes of God, they had as much value as the eagle, the noblest of all birds.

In one Audubon Society's summer bird count, nearly 9,000 of them were spotted across Indiana—second only to starlings and the red-winged blackbirds (which I don't think have become familiar enough to many of us.) I suspect there would have been more counted, but most birdwatchers I know try hard to ignore them. Today sparrows, along with starlings, are considered pests. They are messy, pushy, not so pretty, and noisy. They don't build beautiful nests like other birds. They just kind of throw them together. They don't have a beautiful song like other birds either. They're just around in plentiful numbers—and only God knows why.

That's what makes the words of Jesus so surprising: " Yet not one of them will fall to the ground apart from your Father." (Mt 10:29). Literally, that means "without the knowledge of God." Luke says it a bit differently: "Yet not one of them is forgotten in God's sight" (Lk 12:6). The New International Version translates it as "apart from the will of your Father." That has always bothered me because it sounds as if God wills the death of his creatures. I prefer the translations that say God watches what naturally happens; God doesn't cause it.

But even the hairs of your head are all counted.

One of the most incisive descriptions of what happens when the sparrow falls to the ground is in a bit of dialogue from Mary Doria Russell's novel, *The Sparrow*.

> "So, God just leaves?" John asked, angry where Emilio had been desolate. "Abandons creation? You're on your own, apes. Good luck!"
> "No. He watches. He rejoices. He weeps. He observes the moral drama of human life and gives meaning to it by caring passionately about us, and remembering."
> "Matthew ten, verse twenty-nine," Vincenzo Giuliani said quietly. "Not one sparrow can fall to the ground without your Father knowing it."
> "But the sparrow still falls," Felipe said.[1]

God knows. God does not always prevent.

One translation suggests that the word we say is "fall" is better rendered "light" upon the ground. That means that God watches the sparrow every time it lands and hops on the ground—not just when it "drops dead." God cares about them, but God also cares *for* them. In another place, Jesus said that God feeds the birds of the air. People in Jesus' day believed that. The one hundred thirty-sixth Psalm begins by telling the story about the God

[1] Mary Doria Russell, *The Sparrow*, (New York: Ballantine Books, 2008), 401.

who is the God of creation, then it goes on to tell the story about the God who is the God of history, the God who rescued Israel from Egypt and who fought her battles for her; then finally it goes on to speak of God as the God who "gives food to all flesh" (Psalm 136:25). For sure, the God who created the world is the God who prepares lunch! From the creation of the universe to the provision of our daily bread, God's love for us is evident.

The affirmation that God pays attention to the worthless sparrow led Jesus to say something else that is a bit startling. "But even the hairs of your head are all counted" (Lk 12:7). God not only knows when the sparrows hop or drop dead, God has such intimate knowledge of us that God keeps track of how many hairs we have on our heads. (That doesn't take much effort when it comes to some of us; God is having fewer to worry about all the time!) The average head has 100,000 to 120,000 hairs. We lose about 40-100 of them every day. You might also be interested to know that in winter, a house sparrow has over 3,500 feathers. I would guess Jesus could have gone on to say that God has counted the feathers on those sparrows.

I remember reading a devotional by a resident of the Philippines who said he wondered who had been motivated enough to count the one thousand islands in his nation, or the seven thousand islands in the Malay Archipelago. He said for some reason it seemed important to someone. The truth is, we do keep track of and count and number the things that are important to us. We know batting averages, stock market quotes, and our golf score. We know miles per gallon. We keep track of calories, blood pressure readings and our cholesterol. And in the same way, God keeps count of the hairs of our head. Probably even the wrinkles on our faces.

I think Jesus was saying several things. God is so intimately aware of each of us that God knows how many hairs we have. We don't even know that about ourselves. And God is also intensely concerned when we lose our hair because of stress. Or chemotherapy. God knows which ones have been colored to avoid showing our gray. God knows which ones we pull out at work. God cares about what we care about.

The psalmist meditates on the fact God had intimate knowledge of us:

> O LORD, you have searched me and known me.
> You know when I sit down and when I rise up; you discern my thoughts from far away.

> You search out my path and my lying down and are acquainted with all my ways.
> Even before a word is on my tongue, O LORD, you know it completely. (Ps 139:1-4)

That means God treats us as incredibly unique. Every single one of us. We can never be lost in a crowd in God's eyes. That also means each of us is different. The thing about God's creation is that there is no such thing as mass production. Each person shows the handiwork of the Creator. We are all originals. Just like every snowflake is different.

Jesus was telling the disciples that for a reason. He was sending them out for their mission in a hostile world. He compared it to being like sheep in the midst of wolves. He told them not to fear those who kill the body but cannot kill the soul. He told them they did not need to fear persecution and suffering. He told them not to be afraid, because they were of more value than many sparrows.

He was also giving us something to remember when we feel pretty insignificant, like sparrows. Ordinary or average. Like one of the little people. Like when we are laid off during our company's downsizing. When we are overlooked when the all-star awards are passed out, or the team chosen. When we're always a bridesmaid and never a bride. When other people are picked for promotions.

We really wonder if God has the time or interest to keep track of our petty problems. We wonder if God cares when we are caught in the storms of life. You'll remember when the disciples were out in the boat with Jesus and a great windstorm came up and the waves swamped the boat, but Jesus slept in the stern and they had to wake him up and ask him, "Teacher, do you not care that we are perishing?" (Mk 4:38). Their question is ours: "Wake up, God, don't you care what I'm going through?"

We wonder if God cares when we begin to pray. Does God really hear our prayers? When I was growing up, I could never understand how God could listen to several billion people all at once. How could God keep the voices and the requests straight? The older I became, the more I wondered if God could be expected to pay that much attention and hear us all individually. Most of us wonder if God hears our prayers and acts on them. In her book, *Does God Care?* Georgia Harkness discusses the meaning of the providence of God, which she calls the belief that God looks after us, with goodness and guidance, with sustaining care. She said that belief depends upon faith in a personal God. "Only a personal God can know or care what happens to persons." She says one of the arguments against such a belief is the vastness of the universe and the relative insignificance of each individual human life.[2] That's the question raised in the eighth Psalm:

When I look at your heavens, the work of your fingers,
the moon and the stars that you have established;
what are human beings that you are mindful of them,
mortals that you care for them? (Ps 8:3-4)

When I look at the vast universe, I can't help but wonder, who are we that God should care for us? Can God be trusted to hear, care, and act for our good?

I think one of the reasons we end up so anxious and worrying so much of the time is that we have never come to the point when we believe God cares about us. Maybe we could take a lesson from the birds. In the mid-nineteenth century, Elizabeth Cheney wrote the familiar poem, "Overheard in An Orchard."

Said the Robin to the Sparrow,
"I should really like to know
why these anxious human beings
rush about and worry so?"
Said the Sparrow to the Robin,
"Friend, I think that it must be
that they have no heavenly Father
such as cares for you and me."

The truth is, most of the time we act as if we have no heavenly Father who cares for us, don't we? The First Letter of Peter reminds us, "Cast all your anxiety on him, because he cares for you" (I Pet 5:7). Jesus spoke often of our need to be less anxious, and it was always in the context of trusting God.

We are not the only ones who may feel like sparrows. Others do, too. That's why Jesus' lesson is an important one. If God notices them and cares about them, shouldn't we? I've always been impressed with the kinds of people that caught Jesus' attention. Zacchaeus is a good example.

[2] Georgia Harkness, *Does God Care?*, (Waco: Word Books, 1960), 18-19.

Jesus was always looking for and paying attention to the least, the lost, the left-out. The people who were considered "the others," those who faded into the woodwork, the common folk, the outsiders.

Lee Strobel says we might read the Bible like an adoption ad in the paper: God would write something like, "I'll take the person who feels inadequate and mediocre. I'll take the unworthy...I'll take the person whose misguided quest for fulfillment has gotten her mired in immorality. I'll take the person who's struggling with unanswered question. I'll take the person who's on the treadmill of trying to prove she's *somebody*."[3]

Mother Teresa built her ministry on that. She said needy persons feel devalued. But in the eyes of God, every single individual has infinite value and is worthy of being treated with dignity and respect. She liked to say, "Our poor are very great people."

No one should feel completely alone. That is why God gave us the church. We are those who care for and look after the *sparrow people*. A student once asked anthropologist Margaret Mead for the earliest sign of civilization in a given culture. He expected the answer to be a clay pot or perhaps a fishhook or grinding stone. Instead, her answer was: "A healed femur." Dr. Mead explained that no mended bones are found where the law of the jungle, survival of the fittest, reigns. A healed femur shows that someone cared. Someone had to do that injured person's hunting and gathering until the leg healed. The evidence of compassion is the first sign of civilization.

I decided I'd look in some of my bird books about sparrows. To see if, in fact, they have any redeemable qualities—other than eating the Japanese Beetles that bug most all of us. One book I have on bird behavior, by Donald Stokes, begins the chapter on sparrows with "You will find the house sparrow an engaging subject for behavior-watching once you start to take an interest in distinguishing its various calls and watching its interactions with its own and other species."[4] In some neighborhoods, it may be the only bird some people ever see—except for starlings and pigeons. And if you look closely, the male is not really that unattractive, with its brown back, white wing bars, and black bib. The English sparrow, or house sparrow, is not a sparrow but a weaver finch. They were brought to this country in 1850 to eat the canker worms on trees in city parks. Just like with the starling, that theory backfired and the one thought to take care of pests became a pest. I did learn that the English

[3] Lee Strobel, *What Would Jesus Say?*, (Grand Rapids: Zondervan, 1994), 26.

[4] Donald Stokes, *A Guide to Bird Behavior Volume* I, 261.

sparrow is a good husband and father, helping build the bulky nest, helping a bit with incubation of the eggs, and helping out a lot with feeding the young. They are homebodies. Unlike most other birds, they don't just use their nests for a few weeks at a time, but year-round. They are monogamous for life.

I also learned house sparrows are very expressive birds and one of their many behaviors is one that seems to have the same meaning as saying "please." Young birds beg for food by crouching, lifting their bills, spreading and lowering their wings and quivering them. Since that behavior is typical of adult sparrows as well, as when a male wants a female to try out a nest site, scientists are pretty sure it means "please."

I guess one of the reasons I particularly like sparrows is that compared to other birds, they are oddly human. Or at least like some people I know. They are among the last birds to get up in the morning and the first birds to retire in the evening, and they seem to have lots of time to loaf during the day. They even like to sunbathe. They are great talkers. I am pretty sure you've never heard a sparrow sing. They chirp. They seem to just *converse* with one another.

They are also very social birds. That's because they are descendants of the weaver finches in Africa whose huge colonies number in the thousands. I remember seeing trees in Africa just loaded with coconut-sized balls of straw and grass. Don Stokes writes,

> One of the most intriguing patterns of behavior is their habit of forming large communal roosts at night and during the day. Birds will travel from a distance of up to four miles to join the roost at night. They settle in their primary roost about a half-hour before sunset and leave after sunrise. Around midday they establish a secondary roost, where they sit, preen, and call noisily and continuously. One theory about these roosts is that they are information centers that help birds locate food. In each roost there are birds that have found food and those that haven't. Those without follow those that have to their feeding areas the next day. The larger the roosts, the greater the area surveyed for food and the better the chances of survival for the whole flock.[5]

[5]Ibid. 271-272.

I don't know about you, but to me that sounds like the church! Paul wrote to the Corinthian Church, "Consider your own call, brothers and sisters: not many of you were wise by human standards, not many were powerful, not many were of noble birth..." (I Cor 1:26). What we are, I guess, is just a *communal roost,* and since one of the most basic definitions of evangelism is "one beggar telling another beggar where to find food," I guess what we do in our communal roost is have those who have found food tell those who haven't where it is. And the more of us who come together, the greater area of experience and the better the chances of survival for the whole flock. Sometimes the church looks about as chaotic as a sparrow's nest. Not everything we do is neat and tidy, like the exquisitely woven purses of thc orioles or as tightly constructed as the robin's nest.

Personally, I think that might be okay with God. As has often been said, the church isn't a showplace or museum for perfect people, but a hospital for those who have been wounded and broken in life. I want a church like that. I want it to be a shelter where, as the psalmist said, "even the sparrows find a home."

Questions for Contemplating and Conversing

1. Have you ever felt insignificant? When and why?
2. How do you know God cares about you personally?
3. Do you want your church to be made up of the *movers and shakers,* the *successful and powerful* of your community?
4. How is your church welcoming and accepting of *sparrow people*?
5. What are your thoughts about the dialogue in *The Sparrow*?
6. What is the main lesson you learned from this chapter?

Part Two
Considering Lilies

9. In the Garden

"It may be true that time began in a garden."
-Emilie Barnes

One of the most popular hymns of all time is "In the Garden." It's interesting that Austin Miles sold that song for $4, back in 1912. By the time of his death, the song had been printed more than three million times.

I was once given a copy of a modern-day version of that old hymn: "I Come to the Garden Alone (Because no sane person gets up this early)." Unfortunately, I don't know who wrote it. It begins:

I come to the garden alone
And the aphids are still on the roses
So, I pause to spray and I hope today
The aphid decomposes

The chorus continues:

And I hoe some weeds
And I sow some seeds
And I get a thorn in my toe…

Gardening is America's No. 1 hobby; nearly a $50 billion industry. (William Alexander's humorous book, *The $64 Tomato*, is about his mission to grow the perfect garden, and how the expense of tools, fertilizers, and pesticides, etc., resulted in a cost of $64 per tomato.)

A friend gave me a book of quotations related to gardening, and she included a note which said, "Who loves a garden, still his Eden keeps."

There's nothing better than working in the dirt. In fact, that's an image I have of God, in the very beginning—with dirty hands. That's how the poet James Weldon Johnson described the creation:

> Up from the bed of the river
> God scooped the clay;
> And by the bank of the river
> He kneeled him down;
> And there the great God Almighty
> Who lit the sun and fixed it in the sky,
> Who flung the stars to the most far corner of the night,
> Who rounded the earth in the middle of his hand;
> This great God,
> Like a mammy bending over her baby,
> Kneeled down in the dust
> Toiling over a lump of clay
> Till he shaped it in is his own image;
> Then into it he blew the breath of life,
> And man became a living soul.
> Amen. Amen.[1]

That might be the reason children are drawn to the dirt! They can spend hours just *getting dirty*. Why not? They are imitating God, going back to the beginning of time. The image of God in us may be most fully expressed when we *scoop up* and *toil over a lump of clay.*

It is right there in the first book of the Bible, Genesis: Soon after the creation of the earth and sky, day and night, God created a *garden.* Not a beach, not a road, not a city teeming with commerce. A garden. "Then God said, 'Let the earth put forth vegetation: plants yielding seed, and fruit trees of every kind on earth that bear fruit with the seed in it.' And it was

[1] James Weldon. Johnson, "The Creation," *African American Literature: A Brief Introduction and Anthology*, Al Young (ed.), (New York: HarperCollins College Publishers, 1996), 369-72.

so" (Gen 1:11). There it was: "And the LORD God planted a garden in Eden, in the east; and there he put the man whom he had formed" (Gen 2:8). Adam became the world's first gardener. "The LORD God took the man and put him in the garden of Eden to till it and keep it" (Gen 2:15).

In the view of theologian Paul Tillich, God is the "ground of being." Tillich resisted any idea of "objectifying God," and identified God rather as the basis of ultimate reality. God is the Beginning. God underlies everything. God is the Firm Foundation of all of life.

The "ground" is also the surface of the earth, the soil and rock. That may be the place where many of us experience God. Like the little plaque in my garden puts it, we may "feel nearer to God's heart in a garden than any other place on earth." Soil may be good for the soul.

So much that happened in the Bible took place in a garden.

It was in the Garden of Eden that Adam and Eve learned how good and beautiful were the things that God had provided for God's world, but also that there are certain "don't-do-that's" associated with enjoying them. As a consequence of their disobedience, Adam and all of us since were condemned to toil and to till the earth, constantly having to wage war against thorns and thistles when we seek to restore God's gift of a once lush and abundant garden.

Jesus went to a garden the night before his crucifixion to spend time in prayer. It was in a garden that he was laid to rest after his death on the cross. The resurrection took place in that garden.

Jesus' great decision in Gethsemane ultimately reopens the door to what God initially desired at the original Eden for all—a willingness to do God's will. Here, Jesus, the "last Adam" (1 Cor 15:45), reversed the first Adam's errant example by crying out: "He said, 'Abba, Father, for you all things are possible; remove this cup from me; yet, not what I want, but what you want'" (Mk 14:36).

In Revelation 22, we are ushered into a garden-like setting, the ultimate Eden. Here is the New Jerusalem come down from heaven. "Then the angel showed me the river of the water of life, bright as crystal…On either side of the river is the tree of life with its twelve kinds of fruit…and the leaves of the tree are for the healing of the nations" (Rev 22:1-2).

A garden was a place for new beginnings, both at Creation and at Easter. It was a place of decision-making, struggles, yielding to the will of God. It is a symbol of life, new life, and forever-after life.

A garden can simply be a place of pure joy. Few spaces on earth are as beautiful as a flower garden. Longwood Gardens in Pennsylvania, with a collection of 9,000 species and varieties of plants in a 1,000- acre display, had a million-and-a-half visitors in a recent year. Nearly 900 species of native Texas plants grow in the Lady Bird Johnson Wildflower Center in Austin. Both are on every gardener's bucket list.

The *lilies* Jesus pointed to were more likely the *poppy anemone.* They would have been the wildflower better suited to the description Jesus gave and more familiar to his listeners. Regardless, Jesus prized flowers as signs of God's creation and creative power.

It's not just that I find planting and tending a garden a pleasant hobby and a wonderful way to provide beauty, I have always felt that to spend our time doing that, is to do what God wants us to do and to be where God wants us to be. We realize that the outdoors is our natural home as we work alongside God to re-create our own little Gardens of Eden.

Questions for Contemplating and Conversing

1. The legendary British horticulturalist, Gertrude Jekyll, wrote. "Most of all, for me, a garden is a schoolroom. A garden is a grand teacher. It teaches patience and careful watchfulness; it teaches industry and thrift; above all it teaches entire trust." What else can we learn while gardening?
2. Why do you think the Bible begins and ends with scenes of gardens?
3. In what ways are gardens places of creation, decision, resurrection, recreation and re-creation?
4. We know Jesus spent a lot of time outdoors. Do you think Paul did also—since he made several references to planting? Or would most people in that day have a knowledge of gardening since they lived in an agrarian society?
5. Have you ever taken the time to "stop and smell the roses," and to *study* them?
6. What is the main lesson you learned from this chapter?

10. Lessons Learned

"Today I have come to Jalama Beach with the intention of studying the book of nature to see what the Lord might teach me."

-Richard Foster[1]

A member of the church told me she needed to schedule a counseling session with me. She indicated it was pretty urgent. When we made contact a short time later, here is what she asked me: "Bill, I want to plant some tomatoes in a container. What kind of soil should I use?" I should not have been surprised that she wanted to counsel with me about plants. Throughout my ministry, I suspect I have had more questions about vegetables than the virgin birth, soil than souls, plant growth than church growth. In one church, while the associate pastor was teaching a Bible Study class, I was holding sessions on how to force tulips into bloom during the winter months.

In a way, it didn't bother me that I was the go-to person for gardening questions, not just theological ones. I probably paid more attention to

[1] Richard Foster, *Sanctuary of the Soul*, (Downers Grove: IVP Books, 2011), 140-141.

what was growing in my garden than I did to my seminary professors. Henri Amiel said, "A modest garden contains, for those who know how to look and to wait, more instructions than a library."

Since my days of spending summers and working with my grandfather Schwein, the garden has been a virtual classroom for me. Somehow his great wisdom seemed to come attached to something we were doing in the garden or in the greenhouse. I learned a lot of down-to-earth philosophy from him. Flowers were often metaphors for the larger lessons of life. I always thought he saw life differently, and maybe that was because he took the time to pause and reflect on things. Ever since, I think I've learned more about life in the garden than in any school I've attended. I have realized the truth of a line from "The Oak" by James Russell Lowell: "Lord! All Thy works are lessons…" To paraphrase Robert Fulghum, *All I Really Need to Know I Learned in A Garden.* Let me tell you about some of the things I've learned.

First, I have looked, and learned that what God wants more than anything else, is for creation to be restored to its original beauty and goodness. Not all gardening is recreation; it is also re-creation. I think much of what we gardeners do is attempt to re-create the Garden of Eden, where everything was good and bountiful and beautiful. Just right. There is so much ugliness, so much evil in the world. As has been said, "Every rose is an autograph from the hand of God on his world about us."

The writer of Ecclesiastes wrote that "there is a time to plant, and a time to pluck up what is planted" (Eccl 3:2). We live in a day when it feels like most everything has been torn up, torn apart, uprooted, turned upside down. It's past time when we should work on replanting. Ezekiel includes a promise from God that the time would come when people will see: "This land that was desolate has become like the garden of Eden…" (Ezek 36:35). He said God "replanted that which was desolate" (Ezek 36:36). God moves us from desolation to restoration.

I do not know the source of it, but I was struck by a quote that said, "There are so many gardens of life in which no flower blooms anymore, and no bird sings, and in which the fruit of charity will never ripen again. Come and let these barren gardens be replanted, for God wants flowers to bloom and birds to sing in them again and the fruits of love to thrive."

In the early twentieth century, an old shepherd in the South of France lived in a very desolate area. It was devoid of trees, wildlife was gone, water holes had dried up. All the other residents had given up on it. But this old shepherd faithfully planted oaks, hazelnuts, and chestnuts. One day a young man happened on the old man and asked him, “What in the world are you doing, anyway?” “Well, it’s pretty obvious what I’m doing; I’m planting trees.” “But it will be years before these trees will do you any good!” “Yes, but some day they’ll do somebody some good, and they’ll help restore this dry land. I may never see it, but perhaps my children will.”

In the conclusion to this story, the young man returns to the area after fighting in the First World War. He is surprised to see all sorts of saplings taking root in the valley, with streams running through them. The old shepherd had turned it into a Garden of Eden, vibrant with life, more than 10,000 people living there.[2]

It’s up to us to fill the world with beauty and all that’s good. We get glimpses of how it should be when we spend time in our gardens. I was visiting a woman, dying of cancer, who lived in a wooded area, surrounded by the flowers she had planted and those growing wild, and she told me, "I live in a Garden of Eden. Every day is a miracle. Life is beautiful."

At the very least, we should be willing to remind people that there is always “beauty and joy” to be found in life. There is so much ugliness. Sameness. Then, perhaps, to help them find it. Sometimes that might just mean we encourage them to stop and look at flowers. You know the keen power of observation that Sherlock Holmes had. In one of the books in the series, his companion, Dr. Watson, observes how Holmes stopped to study a rose. The detective said, “Our highest assurance of the goodness of Providence seems to me to rest in the flowers…this rose is an extra. Its smell and its color are an embellishment of life…It is only goodness which gives extras, and so I say again that we have much to hope from the flowers.” We are always to be on the lookout for God’s extras.

That doesn't mean our gardens of Eden stay that way without work. Rudyard Kipling once said, "Gardens are not made by singing, 'Oh, how beautiful!' and sitting in the shade."

The second thing I’ve learned is that making life as we want it, and as God wants it, takes lots of effort. One gardener wrote that if you’re in love with a garden, “you’re in hate with everything that threatens it. Gardening forces you to choose sides.” A friend gave me a little sign to place in my little vegetable patch which announced, "Garden of Weedin'." Anyone with a garden of any size knows that to be true. So much of what we do

[2] Jean Giono, *The Man Who Planted Trees*, (United States: Chelsea Green Publishing, 2007).

in the garden we have to do in life. The thing about gardens--and about life--is that you have to pay attention and keep a constant vigil.

Gardening has taught me that life is a mixture of bad and good. Those of us who are into gardening realize it's a life-long war against weeds, bugs, drought, moles, and other things like that. Dag Hammarskjold observed that we can't make a garden and reserve one part of it for weeds.[3] Weeds invade the lawn and flower beds, and before long they take over—if they're not dealt with. I have a good friend who published a gardening newsletter for a number of years, and in one issue she wrote:

> Keeping watch. A close eye. On the lookout. An ounce of prevention is worth a pound of cure…The more we garden, the more obvious the concept: if we notice and deal with small problems in June, while mornings are fresh and cool, the sun is bright and our gardens are still under control, then we can often prevent larger blights and infestations from developing…So much of gardening is devoted to doing. Pruning, clipping, planting, tending, picking, pulling, thinning, clearing…regular inspections help you maintain the upper hand more often than not.

Shakespeare said, "Now 'tis the spring, and weeds are shallow-rooted; Suffer them now and they'll o'er grow the garden."

So many of life's difficulties can be avoided if we "nip them in the bud." Gardening isn't just about what we put in, but what we keep out. What we have to say "no" to. Left to ourselves, with no cultivation, attention, painful pruning and wearisome weeding, we naturally would become overgrown with less-than-desirable aspects of life. It's always better to deal with the little problems before they have a chance to grow and take over. That's true in our marriages. We let little grievances and grudges grow until they become conflict and escalate into war. That's true with bad habits. That's true when we let our children get by with small offenses and breaking lesser rules.

I have a theory about weeds that I want you to verify from your own experience. The weeds that get tangled with my flowers look exactly like the flower leaves. The weeds next to the lobelia plants look exactly like the lobelia. The tall grass with broad leaves prefers to grow next to the

[3] Dag Hammarskjöld, *Markings*, (New York: Alfred A. Knopf, 1965), 15

iris. I have to stand and stare for a long time trying to decide which is which. Even then, when I reached down to pull up a big clump of wild grass, I'd get a handful of iris leaves. The weeds that resemble phlox have somehow managed to congregate in the midst of the phlox. All through the coral bells are otherwise unknown weeds that you cannot tell from coral bells. I'm amazed at this chameleon-like characteristic of the weeds in my garden. Even poison ivy looks a lot like the Virginia creeper it invades. I once had a bed of beautiful St. John's Wort; growing among them were milkweeds. The similarity was uncanny.

For me, that means I need to learn this lesson in life: Sometimes evil is indistinguishable from good. It can cleverly disguise itself. How much easier life would be if it were always possible for us to tell one from the other. Vice often comes looking a lot like virtue. And just like weeds grow in our gardens, evil can find its way into the church. I've been involved in enough conversations with struggling pastors over the years that I'm pretty well convinced that there is a force of evil at work in some of our congregations. You may call it Satan, the devil, whatever—but the truth is, there is a power that is hostile to life, hostile to God, hostile to anything good. Life is a battleground between good and evil.

What is our primary task? Planting seeds or pulling weeds? Have you listened to preachers and religious groups that only talk about what they are against--and wondered, with me, what they are for? We are to concentrate our energies on the positive as a safeguard from making bad judgment calls. I don't know anyone who has much of a yard or a garden and who only pays attention to the weeds. A Master Gardener I know always advises the best way to rid your lawn of weeds is to let the grass grow thicker and taller. Translate that into life, and perhaps the best way to rid the world of evil is to intensify our efforts at doing good. Let the good crowd out the bad. Spend more time planting seeds than pulling weeds. Pull as many weeds as you can, and you'll never create a garden or lawn. Only the planting of seeds will do that. Weeds often just fill in a neglected area. I read that a million dollars spent on incarcerating repeat felons prevents 61 serious crimes, while a million dollars spent on high-school graduation incentives prevents 258 serious crimes.

I have a couple products in my garage which are not bad analogies for the task of the church. One is "Garden Weed Preventer" which promises to prevent weeds before they can germinate and take root. Do you remember the proverb, "An ounce of prevention is worth a pound of cure"? The other is "Weed 'n' Feed," which is not a bad idea, either, for we are to create an environment in which weeds find it hard to germinate and take root, but also to feed and nourish everything that is good.

A minister friend of mine talked about a former All-American basketball player in his congregation who continued to play pick-up games long after his career had ended. The fellow was a good man and was bothered by the language and off-color stories he heard from those with whom he played. He was not the kind of man who would insult or embarrass them or put them down in public. So, he started singing "Amazing Grace" in the locker room one day. Nothing else; he just sang that hymn. Something happened to change the whole environment. He had made a subtle, but powerful, statement about who he was and what he stood for. From that time on, he reported, there was not another curse word uttered or off-color joke told.

Wouldn't it be wonderful if all of the good and beautiful things of life began to crowd out and overtake the bad? If the voices of reason, tolerance, and understanding began to drown out the shouts of hatred and prejudice? May you and I be the ones who continue to sow the good seed in the world.

Though we have no biblical evidence of it, I suspect the Apostle Paul spent time in the gardens of the Mediterranean world. And it was there he learned a great spiritual truth, that whatever it is we sow, that is exactly what we can count on reaping. That’s the third thing I’ve learned: You are only going to harvest what you plant. And plan for. Nothing more, nothing less, nothing else. Paul might have watched farmers plant wheat and wait for it to come up. They didn’t wait for corn, but for wheat. He might have watched gardeners plant apple seeds and wait for apple trees to come up. Not for acorns, but for apples. In observing that, Paul learned one of the basic truths of life, which he wrote to the Galatian Christians: you reap what you sow.

Some of us forget that. We are too shortsighted to see the ways things are bound to work out. If you don't believe that, just re-read Aesop's fable of the Grasshopper and the Ants. You can't spend your whole summer singing and expect to have any corn stored up for winter. We pay tomorrow for our laziness today. We seldom realize how we set the patterns of our lives, make deep ruts that become so difficult to get out of. There is always a day of reckoning, when bills come due, when we will reap what we have sown.

One fellow I knew reminisced about his experiences in the family garden. He said he and his brothers were to plant black-eyed peas one spring. They did pretty well until they began to wish they could go fishing. The more seed peas they dropped, the more there seemed to be. They didn't think they'd ever get done in time to go fishing, so they came up with a plan. When they came to the end of a long row, they hastily dug a hole in the soft earth, pouring in a half-gallon of peas into the hole, covering it up with a mound of dirt. And off they went to go fishing. Three weeks later, their father called them back to the field to see how, at the end of the long row, there were hundreds of tiny plants crowding each other, proclaiming for all to see why there had not been enough peas to finish the planting that spring.

Paul also saw the relationship between the number of seeds sown and the number of plants grown. "The point is this: the one who sows sparingly will also reap sparingly, and the one who sows bountifully will also reap bountifully" (II Cor 9:6). That seems obvious enough, but we don't always act as if we remember it. It's not just a great verse for a stewardship sermon. We are planting seeds everyday of our lives. The things we say and do. The things we don't say and don't do. There's a saying that puts it, "All the flowers of all the tomorrows are in the seeds of today." Many a springtime I have walked around our yard wishing I'd planted tulips and daffodils in the fall. What's on your list of "if-only's" or "I wish I had's," your list of good intentions?

I have also learned a lot about death in the garden. Every fall and winter I am reminded that living things die. Sometimes they die prematurely. No plant lasts forever. But even in the midst of death, there is the promise of resurrection and renewal. Paul apparently learned that, too, because he saw in planting seeds a way to explain the promise of resurrection. In First Corinthians, he answered the question, "How are the dead raised?" by comparing God's promise of resurrection to what happens when a farmer sows an apparently lifeless seed that comes to life again. When it comes to explaining the mystery of the resurrection, I often resort to illustrations and images from the natural world. That is one of the reasons we have tulips and daffodils and lilies at Easter. Flowers die back, but they bloom again.

In Longfellow's words, they are: "Emblems of our own great resurrection / Emblems of the bright and better land." There is no such thing in nature as death having the last word. The noted scientist Werner von Braun once said he believes in immorality because "Science has found that nothing can disappear without a trace. Nature does not know extinction. All it knows is transformation!" He continues:

> Now, if God applies this fundamental principle to the most minute and insignificant parts of His universe, doesn't it make sense to assume that He applies it also to the masterpiece of His creation—the human soul? I think it does. And everything science has taught me—and continues to teach me—strengthen my belief in the continuity of our spiritual existence after death. Nothing disappears without a trace.[4]

The deadest looking bulbs planted in the ground will, in time, burst into bloom. Even little seeds, casually buried in the earth, come back as new creations.

There is a significant verse in John's account of the crucifixion, death and resurrection of Jesus. He said, "Now there was a garden in the place where he was crucified, and in the garden there was a new tomb in which no one had ever been laid" (Jn 19:41). I don't think that was an accident. Gardens are not just places of death, but of new life.

Gardens have taught me about life, about death—and about faith. I don't know how anyone can work in the garden very long without becoming a person of faith. Jesus realized that when he stopped to look at the lilies of the field. They spoke to him of the fact that God provides for us. A gardener wrote that "A gardener works by faith, and often without conscious realization of it." She illustrated that by pointing out that to the outsider, it seems pretty ridiculous to watch a couple drive to a garden center on a late-winter day and spend more than a hundred dollars on a dozen brown sticks labeled "roses." They go home and dig holes in which to place those sticks. She said, "Then they walk away. They have done their part. Now God's earth and sun and rain will do theirs. That's the faith and the trust of a gardener."

We live in a responsive universe. We put a seed in the soil and the world answers back with a flower or a harvest. There is a faithfulness behind the laws of nature. As the hymn puts it, "Great is God's faithfulness…Summer and winter and springtime and harvest…" There is a Superior Intelligence working toward fulfillment of purpose and plan. There is a design and an order to everything around us.

Every seed, bulb or shrub planted is an affirmation of faith. It is an act of confidence that the energy of God will operate through uniform laws to

[4] Wernher von Braun, "Why I Believe in Immortality," in William Nichols (ed.), *The Third Book of Words to Live By*, (New York: Simon and Schuster, 1962) 119-120.

provide sunshine, soil and rain to transform what we do into some thing of beauty or bounty. In a gardening catalogue I once received, there was an anonymous poem:

When I suddenly find I've an axe to grind
With the world and all that's in it,
And I'm sick of life with its grief and strife
And would leave it in a minute;
To ease my hurt—I dig in the dirt
And grapple with lusty weeds,
And chop the sod with a vengeful hoe
And grind a grub with a bitter heel
Into the dust—because I must!
Can you guess how much better it makes me feel?
Then I scatter seeds believing they'll grow,
I KNOW they'll grow…they've done it before,
So—my faith swings back to the proven track
And I am my steady self once more.

There are so many other things I've learned in a garden. I need to spend more time on my knees. Rudyard Kipling wrote, "Adam was a gardener, and God, who made him, sees that half of all good gardening is done upon the knees." (As an aside, I heard of an experiment in Iowa which is attempting to show that plants being prayed over grow much better than those which are not. Thus far, the scientist has claimed an improvement of 40 to 60 percent.) I've learned about giving. Sometimes my plants need to be divided when they become cramped. They need to be shared. That's what somconc has callcd "pass-along plants."

Finally, spending time in the garden taught me about patience, persistence and perseverance. In another of Jesus' parables, he told about the farmer who wanted to cut down a fig tree that hadn't had any fruit on it for three years. But his hired hand protested and said, "Give me another year of working on it; I'll do a little cultivating and fertilizing and then we'll see if that makes any difference. Maybe we've not done all we could for it." (My paraphrase of Lk 13:6-9) Things take time. There's a poem about that:

Put up in a place
Where it's easy to see

The cryptic admonishment
T. T. T.
When you feel how depressingly
Slowly you climb,
It's well to remember that
Things Take Time.[5]

I have seeds that take weeks to germinate and plants that take years to bloom. I have some trees I have been waiting on to bear fruit for years. Things take time. There are times when we can only wait. I have a theory that the more exotic or desirable the plant, the longer it takes to germinate. A marigold will germinate in five days. A cyclamen may take 50 or more days. I think there's a message there: the more desirable the outcome, the longer it may take, and the more patience is required. That can be true with children, situations, and even God's promises.

In the desert Southwest, you can find the century plant. It has leaves up to a foot wide and the plant itself can reach twelve feet in diameter. What makes it unusual, in addition to its size, is that fact that for twenty or thirty years, it stays the same height and puts out no flowers. Then one year, all of a sudden, without a warning, a new bud sprouts. The bud, which resembles a tree-trunk-size asparagus spear, shoots into the sky at a fantastic rate of seven inches per day, reaching a height of twenty to forty feet. Then it crowns itself with several clumps of yellowish blossoms that last up to three weeks.

Good things take time. The first year the Remington Typewriter was on sale, only 8 of them were sold; first year for Coca Cola, only 25 bottles; the VW Beetle, only 330 cars. There may be some seeds of love you've planted which seem to be taking too long to germinate and grow and bear fruit. Don't give up. I learned that in the garden.

I've learned to accept disappointment. One of the most important lessons gardeners learn is how to overcome adversity. Paul said we will reap in time if we do not give up. Gardeners never seem to give up, do they? Season after season. Year after year. Failure after failure. We never give up.

Questions for Contemplating and Conversing

[5] Piet Hein, *Grooks*, (New York: Doubleday and Co., 1969).

1. How could an hour spent working in the garden, or some time spent walking through one, become a *teaching moment* for you? What might you expect to learn?
2. Make a list of what you imagine an avid gardener has learned about life.
3. What are the lessons Jesus wanted us to learn from his *horticultural* parables? (This would be a good time for you to read about the Sower, Matthew 13:3-8; the Weeds, Matthew 13:24-30; the Mustard Seed, Matthew 13:31-32; the Growing Seed, Mark 4:26-29; and the Unfruitful Fig Tree, Luke 13:6-9.
4. Could you write a *horticultural parable?* Try it!
5. What do you do to make the world a better, more beautiful place?
6. What is the main lesson you learned from this chapter?

11. How Does a Garden Grow?

"Mary, Mary, quite contrary,
How does your garden grow?
With silver bells and cockleshells,
And pretty maids all in a row."

-Nursery Rhyme

I've learned maybe everything I need to know. Except one thing. Just HOW does my garden grow? That's not just a question asked in a nursery rhyme.

I wish I understood more about how plants grow. What gives cells the urge and means to divide and multiply themselves? For that matter, how do children "grow like a weed"? I feel like the 5th graders who wrote: "Rainbows are just to look at, not to really understand." "I am not sure how clouds get formed. But the clouds know how to do it, and that is the important thing." "Water vapor gets together in a cloud. When it is big enough to be called a drop, it does." Perhaps one of the reasons Jesus instructed us to become like little children is that they have an approach to life and to the natural world that allows for amazement and mystery. They have a sense of wonder which we ought to envy and emulate. St. Teresa said, "I believe that in each little thing created by God there is more than what is understood."

Jesus told a parable about a man who scattered seed on the ground, went to bed, and after several days, "the seed would sprout and grow, he does not know how." J. B. Phillips translates that: "though he has no idea how it happens" (Mk 4:26-27).[1] Of course he didn't. He knew nothing of germination, cell division, and photosynthesis. Jesus wanted us to see all growth as a miracle. There are powers and resources beyond our comprehension and our control. The natural world could be seen as evidence of the miraculous power of God. And God's providence.

Miracle and mystery. As plants grow, we witness a miracle. When we ask, "How do they do that?" we ponder a mystery. I think one of the reasons I love to grow my own vegetables and flowers from seeds is that I am always amazed at how a small, hard, apparently lifeless object slowly emerges from the dirt as a green plant. I can plant the seeds, but I cannot make them grow. I can only stand aside, waiting and watching, to see what happens next. When a seed sprouts, I get a glimpse of a great mystery. Someone has said "Watching something grow is good for morale. It helps you believe in life." I'd add, it's also good for our faith by helping us believe in God. An old man who had tended a cherry orchard for thirty years told a visitor: "I see my cherry trees in bud and then in flower, and then in fruit. And then, I believe in God." Someone has said that God acts as if the whole world is God's own back yard. I like that.

I'm afraid too many of us in a post-modern world have lost that. The psalmist believed the world was full of God and evidences of God's creative power: "He covers the heavens with clouds, prepares rain for the earth, makes grass grow upon the hills…" (Ps 147:8). We don't think much about how God covers the heavens with clouds and prepares rain for the earth—we watch the Weather Channel to see where the jet stream is headed. Back in the time of Jesus, people didn't know how things happened, so they said it was God who did everything. We know how, now, and we don't mention God. I believe seeing God at work in ways we cannot always understand or perceive or prove is absolutely essential if we are to believe God works in other ways and places. To see growth as a miracle opens us to the miraculous and mysterious ways God works in many other areas of life.

[1] J. B. Phillips, *The New Testament in Modern English*, (New York: The Macmillan Company, 1958), 77.

A minister tells of coming into the sanctuary of his church one Sunday morning and having an imaginary conversation with the flowers on the altar. He said to them, "How lovely you are; how did you do it?" And they answered, "We hardly know. It started a long way off, ninety million miles away, the great sun smiled down. God turned the planet around and said that spring was here. We felt a stirring in our hearts, and all around us within reach of our rootlet fingers we found what we needed. The Heavenly Father had put it there. We reached out and laid hold on God's provision. We trusted in providence, and here we are."

J. B. Phillips translates the sentence about the earth producing a crop, "without any help from anyone (Mk 4:28).[2] Are there some things that happen without our help? And, ultimately, isn't the potential for growth of any kind really up to God? We talk so much in churches today about "church growth." And we work on marketing plans and making our worship more seeker friendly, and we use the media to get the word out. We develop strategies and plans. I think we might also recall what St. Paul wrote to the Corinthians, "So neither the one who plants nor the one who waters is anything, but only God who gives the growth" (I Cor 3:7). Aren't there certain things that only God can do?

The way we see growth as a miracle opens us to the miraculous and mysterious ways God works in other areas of life. There are any number of things that God does without our help, or with limited assistance from us.

I have always been bothered by the fact that about the only time we use the phrase, "an act of God," is when something bad happens: a tornado, a flood, a lightning strike. Are there any "good" acts of God anymore? Isn't the growth of a seed into a plant and then to harvest an "act of God"? And the growth of a congregation: isn't it really an act of God?

I don't know of many places that teach us about being partners with God more eloquently than a garden. It is not only about what we can count on God to do, but also about what God can count on us to do. Ask God for flowers, and God drops a few seeds into your hands. Ask God for bread, and God tells you to go plant some wheat. Anything, even faith, takes effort on our parts.

I think for a lot of us, one of the most important questions to ask is "What's the responsibility of God and what's my responsibility?" There

[2] Ibid. 77.

is no divine catalogue from which you can order ready-to-pick vegetable plants. Anything takes effort. Ignatius of Loyola is quoted as saying, "Pray as if everything depended on God; act as if everything depended on you." I got into a discussion one morning with some other pastors about just how much God is involved and can be counted on to intervene in our lives and world. I wish I could report we came up with a lot of good answers. How does God work in the world? How we answer that might determine what we believe about prayer and how receptive we are to the power beyond ourselves that God offers us.

Are there times we are to answer our own prayers? What's up to us? What's up to God? And what is God up to in our day? Though I will never know just how God does what God does, I know that we are called to be in partnership. We are God's co-workers in the re-creation of his world. That's why God invites you to come into the garden.

Questions for Contemplating and Conversing

1. Think about "miracle and mystery." What all would you place in that category?
2. If you could explain how plants grow scientifically, would that change your idea of what God does?
3. Are you a person who takes things for granted, or do you want to better understand the *how and why* of things?
4. Are there things you have expected God to do that you could have done for yourself?
5. Are there things you have done for yourself that you should have let God do?
6. Make a list of what you believe you can count on God to do.
7. What is the main lesson you learned from this chapter?

12. Who Planted All Those Weeds?

"I learn more about God
From weeds than from roses;
Resilience springing
Through the smallest chink of hope
In the absolute of concrete...."

-Phillip Pulfrey[1]

In a church I once served, I decided I didn't like the artificial pansies in the concrete flower pots at the front of the church. So, I pulled them out and filled the pots with potting soil I brought from home. I was going to plant petunias I had. I went home and got them ready to transplant, but something interrupted me and I didn't get it done right then. The next day, when I finally brought the plants, there were already beautiful mums someone had planted in the pots.

I think most of us wish that's how our gardens appeared. We wish there were more of those random acts of kindness. Unfortunately, there are also random acts of tragedy, suffering and evil. Jesus said they are like weeds

[1] Phillip Pulfrey, "Weeds," Perspectives, www.originals.net.

which show up in surprising ways, unannounced and unforeseen forces that undo all our work and ruin our hopes and dreams. That's what he talked about in a parable:

> "The kingdom of heaven may be compared to someone who sowed good seed in his field; but while everybody was asleep, an enemy came and sowed weeds among the wheat, and then went away. So when the plants came up and bore grain, then the weeds appeared as well. And the slaves of the householder came and said to him, 'Master, did you not sow good seed in your field? Where, then, did these weeds come from?' He answered, 'An enemy has done this.' The slaves said to him, 'Then do you want us to go and gather them?' But he replied, 'No; for in gathering the weeds you would uproot the wheat along with them. Let both of them grow together until the harvest; and at harvest time I will tell the reapers, Collect the weeds first and bind them in bundles to be burned, but gather the wheat into my barn'" (Mt 13:24-30).

We all have our ideas about how things should be. Coffee is ready when we awaken. We lose weight easily. There's only good news on the television. Forest fires are quickly brought under control. The weather forecaster was wrong about tornadoes in our area. The check arrives in the mail. Our son's report card shows only As. The car's air conditioner works and no appliances need repair or replacement.

Only in our dreams does everything go right. In the real world, things go wrong. All the time, it seems.

Most of us would agree that some kind of force is out to thwart every good desire we have in life and every good design God has for our lives. It surely does feel that way, doesn't it? Everything we want to do and try to do, there is an opposing force at work. It's a fact of life. Whatever you do, something is out to work against it. That there is always equal and opposite reaction to every action is not just a law of physics. Make a proposal, and there is going to be a "Devil's advocate" to play the adversarial role. Have a dream, and someone will tell you it cannot be done. My dad taught me early on that church boards existed for only one reason, and that was to vote down anything the minister wanted to do. No matter what great idea someone comes up with, there will always be someone to speak or work against it. Try to do something good, and almost immediately something springs up to kill it. Organize a team to do good and someone is busy putting together a team to compete against you. We end up saying, "Nothing ever goes right. Everything goes wrong."

That's why we know how that farmer in Jesus' story felt. Jesus compared the kingdom of heaven to good seed sowed in a field, "but while everybody was asleep, an enemy came and sowed weeds among the wheat." It's hard to believe, but people in Jesus' day actually did sow weed seeds in their enemies' fields. It was a common method for getting revenge. Even today, in India, one of the most serious threats that one man can make to another is, "I will sow bad wheat in your field."

I don't think any of my "enemies" go to the trouble of sowing weed seeds in my garden, but I have waged a life-long war against weeds in my yard. You probably have, too. It does seem like someone is deliberately planting weeds while we're gone on vacation or we aren't spending enough time in our gardens. Not even this summer's heat and drought seem to reduce their numbers. Columnist Dave Barry once observed that "Crabgrass can grow on bowling balls in airless rooms, and there is no known way to kill it that does not involve nuclear weapons." The same could be said for most every other kind of weed. The weeds invade the lawn and the flower beds, and before long, a garden can become nothing but a wilderness--or jungle.

Weeds, in the Bible, had just as much of a negative connotation as they do for us today. In fact, Jesus considered them to be metaphors for evil. That's why I have thought of this parable in the same way that I question why there is so much suffering in the world. If life is like a garden, and the good things are like the flowers and plants, then surely weeds are like the bad things that happen to good people. You may not know the name of every weed in your yard, but I can assure you that you are familiar with all the bad things that invade our otherwise peaceful and pleasant lives. Airplanes crash, houses burn, trains leave their tracks, ships collide. There are earthquakes, floods, cyclones, hurricanes, tornadoes. Barges crash into bridges, planes are flown into buildings, passengers in cars are killed by falling trees, swimmers bitten by sharks, whole office buildings blown up, floors collapse at weddings, refugees are driven into starvation, innocent people are killed by drive-by shooters, children are kidnapped and murdered, or just left alone in overheated cars. On and on it goes.

There are any number of tragedies more personal and closer to home. I unpacked some more of my books the other day and came across the pastoral record in which I have noted every baptism, wedding, and funeral I've done over my fifty-five years of ministry. I turned to the pages of funerals. There was the name of a young man who drowned. A young man who took his own life. So many who had died of cancer, including my own mother and my only sister. A close friend who took his own life. Premature babies who had died. Babies who died of SIDS. A fifteen-year-old girl who took her own life. Stillborn babies. An 83-year-old man who took his own life. A middle-aged man who died in a boating accident. Much-too-young men and women who died suddenly. A young girl and a young man who died in automobile accidents. A 16-year-old boy who took his own life. Young men who died of AIDS. A young woman who was killed when she was hit by a bus downtown.

That's why this is one of my favorite parables--not just because it's about someone else who had to fight weeds—but because it raises a question I have asked myself and have been asked so many times: "Why are there bad things in life, and where do they come from?" Like Hoover Rupert, who wrote a book titled, *Why Didn't Noah Swat Both Mosquitoes?* I wonder why God hasn't destroyed the weeds. I also wonder why God created them in the first place, if in fact God did. Why didn't God create moles to only eat the roots of weeds? Why is it that life has to be so hard? Who is working against us all the time? When the farmer's servants asked him, "Did you not sow good seed in your field? Where, then, did these weeds come from?" he answered "An enemy has done this." That should be reassuring to those who wonder if God is responsible for the existence of evil. God never intends evil, not even to test us, or tempt us, or to teach us hard work. The farmer says, "An enemy has done this." Who is that enemy--and where did HE come from? This parable addresses the question of why--if we have a good God who created a good world--is there evil and suffering?

When we address the "problem of evil," we can speak of natural evil and moral evil--the difference between falling into a well or getting pushed into a well--but even that leads to the question, as old as creation, "When God created the world, why was evil a part of it? Where did the serpent--the personalization of evil--come from? Who dropped him off in the Garden of Eden? Or who let him in?"

I can only answer with, "I don't know." Jesus didn't speculate on the origin of evil. Like the book of Job, this passage leaves us with so many unanswered questions. Parables were never meant to say everything that can be said about an issue. Jesus simply wanted us to know that there is a power that is hostile to life, hostile to God, hostile to everything that is good. We may call that power Satan, the devil, the tempter, whatever, but the truth is, life is a battleground between good and evil.

In his book, *The People Of The Lie*, M. Scott Peck admits he had difficulty labeling the existence of evil. He said it is not a scientific term but comes from the pre-enlightenment worldview that supernatural forces controlled human destiny. Yet he came to the conclusion that evil is the only way to describe the force that influences some people he sees in counseling. He once turned to his son and asked him to define evil. His son said, "Evil is 'live' spelled backwards." That is how Peck explains evil: evil is the opposite of life. It is what destroys life.[22]

Does Satan exist and can we blame him for sin and evil? All I'm sure of is that evil exists. Even in me. Aleksandr Solzhenitsyn reminds us,

> Gradually it was disclosed to me that the line separating good and evil passes not through states, nor between classes, nor between political parties either—but right through every human heart—and through all human hearts. This line shifts. Inside us, it oscillates with the years. And even within hearts overwhelmed by evil, one small bridgehead of good is retained. And even in the best of all hearts, there remains… an unuprooted small corner of evil.[33]

It would seem to follow, then, that our task in the Church is to weed out the evil. But this story issues an important word of caution to those who would be too zealous in their crusades and witch hunts. In Palestine, the weeds were called tares, or darnel, which is a poisonous weed. In the early stages of growth, it is hard to distinguish it from wheat. Then, as the crop grows, the black weeds stand out against the golden grain, but it becomes impossible to separate the darnel from the wheat. The roots become intertwined. If you pull the weed, you uproot the wheat. You could burn off the whole field and sow again, but usually the farmer left them to grow together until the time of harvest when the wheat was then separated from the weeds by hand.

The seeds of the tare are highly susceptible to a poisonous hallucinogenic fungus. It could ruin a crop and poison livestock and people. No wonder the servants felt it was urgent to get rid of the awful stuff as quickly as possible. Otherwise, the infected tare seed would

[2] M. Scott Peck, *People of the Lie*, (United States: Touchstone, 1983), 42.
[3] Alexandr Solzhenitsyn, *The Gulag Archipelago, Vol. 2*, (New York Harper & Row, 1974), 617.

become mixed in with the good grain. It would potentially ruin the next year's crop.

Jesus warned against the natural "urge to purge" most all of us have, for, as he said, "In gathering the weeds you would uproot the wheat along with them." Like the Pharisees who wanted to weed-out those who gathered about Jesus whom they labeled sinners, too often all we accomplish is successfully destroying the good right along with the bad. Some of those so-called sinners we might later come to call "saints." I once heard it suggested that if we get rid of the weed-like people, we will miss something that God always does: turn weeds into wheat, which is conversion. And I don't think we can manage to rid the world of evil when we cannot root it out in ourselves.

Abraham Lincoln once said, "There are few things wholly evil or wholly good. Almost everything is an inseparable compound of the two." There are no 100% pure people or totally bad people.

There's another thing about the difficulty we have in separating the good from the bad in life. Not only do weeds reduce the quality and quantity of plants by competing with them for sunlight, water, and nourishment from the soil—and march through the garden like Hitler moving through Poland--but (as I noted in a previous chapter) they have this incredible ability to closely resemble the very flowers they are conquering.

Just as the farmer in the parable told his servants to let the wheat and tares grow together until the harvest, that's a way of saying, "Beware of making those judgments." It has been said that we are to be cultivators, not harvesters. Nor are we judge and jury. That's God's job. God allows the evil to exist and grow along with the good--for the present. But that does not mean there is not a time when they are separated. In the end, at the time of harvest, God will handle the problem of evil. It is God's prerogative, not ours. It is not our job to decide who belongs to the kingdom or to weed out those who do not. The farmer promised that the weeds would be destroyed, and he, not the servants, would determine which is wheat and which are weeds. Essentially, this is a parable of hope: eventually evil-doers will receive their punishment.

For one thing, that should discourage us from labeling people. Ralph Waldo Emerson has said, "What is a weed? A plant whose virtues have not yet been discovered." I once asked the lady in charge of providing altar flowers in my church to go out in the fields and gather some of what most of us would dismiss as a weed patch. She made quite a striking altar arrangement that next Sunday.

Horticulturists define a weed as a plant that is out of place. In one of his books, Robert Fulghum talks about living next door to one of those immaculate people whose yard looked like a golf course. One day he caught his neighbor in his yard spraying dandelions.

The man said, "Didn't really think you'd mind." "Mind, mind!--you just killed my flowers," Fulghum yelled with contempt. His neighbor told him they weren't flowers, but weeds. "Weeds," Fulghum said, "are plants growing where people don't want them. In other words, weeds are in the eye of the beholder. And as far as I am concerned, dandelions are not weeds--they are flowers." He went on to say that he likes them because they cover his yard "with no help from him at all, they mind their own business, they are resistant to disease, bugs, heat, cold, wind, rain, and human beings. If they were rare and fragile, people would knock themselves out to pay $14.95 a plant, raise them by hand in greenhouses, and form dandelion societies."[4]

If we remembered that weeds are in the eye of the beholder, that might save us from making those bad calls which destroy weeds which can turn out to be flowers. Growing native plants is the latest vogue in landscape design. Foreign or exotic plants are condemned as alien invaders or aggressive intruders. It does not take much of a stretch to understand how a good many people feel that way about their nation or community. The leading landscape architect in Nazi Germany was the most radical promoter of native plants and in 1941 German landscape architects proposed a law forbidding the use of foreign plants. They even called for the extermination of a small forest plant that was seen as a stranger and a competitor to native plants.

Sound familiar? At the very least, this is a parable which encourages tolerance and acceptance of what is different and unfamiliar. Native plants are preferred to foreign ones. The only "true" culture is a native one. In Nazi Germany, the superiority of the German people was part of their national identity. Hence, German gardens were predominant. National landscapes and native plants reflected racist, nationalistic values. Foreign plants were eliminated. "Our feelings for our homeland should be rooted in the character of domestic landscape," said one landscape architect.

[4] Robert Fulghum, *All I Ever Need to Know I Learned in Kindergarten*, (New York: Villard Books, 1988), 67-68

Instead of reacting against evil, excising it from our midst once it is discovered, the farmer instructs his servants to work for the good's benefit. We are to be in the business of doing good, taking positive measures, nurturing the good even if it has to exist in the midst of evil and is always in danger of being overcome by it.

There's one other way we are warned against premature labeling an experience as either good or bad. A farmer had one horse and one son. One day his horse broke out of the corral and fled to the freedom of the hills. A neighbor came that night and said, "Your horse got out? That's too bad." "Why?" asked the farmer, "How do you know it's bad?" Sure enough, the next night the horse came back to his familiar corral for his usual feeding and watering, leading twelve wild stallions with him. Suddenly they had thirteen horses instead of none. The neighbor heard the good news and came immediately. "Oh, so now you have thirteen horses! That's good!" The farmer answered, "How do you know that's good?" Days later, his young son was trying to break one of the wild stallions only to be thrown off and break a leg. The neighbor came back that night and passed judgment, "Your son broke his leg? That's sure too bad! The farmer answered yet again, "How do you know it's bad?" Sure enough, a few days later a representative of the army came to town and conscripted every able-bodied young man, taking them off to war. But the farmer's young son was exempted because of his broken leg.

It often takes a much longer view to adequately judge whether something is good or bad. Don't forget that, in time, the day on which Jesus was crucified began to be called *Good* Friday.

Questions for Contemplating and Conversing

1. Have you been guilty of premature judgments about what is good or what is bad?
2. Have there been events and experiences in your life which, in time, have changed from bad to good?
3. In what ways are you a mixture of good and evil?
4. Where does evil come from?
5. How has your life reflected efforts to eradicate evil?
6. What is the main lesson you learned from this chapter?

13. I'd Rather Be a Weed

"The ubiquitous nature of weeds can make them seem like they can grow anywhere, and that's because they can."

I know. I've been rather negative about weeds up to now. But as I've also noted, they have their good side. It might be a fun get-acquainted game, or psychological test, to ask what kind of *plant* we'd like to be. I am certainly not a Sweet William, and I never liked being called a pansy. I suppose I'd like to be a perennial rather than an annual. But to be quite honest, I'd rather be a weed. After all, as Isaiah noted, "The grass withers, the flower fades…" (Isaiah 40:7). Weeds seem to be forever.

Several years ago, a friend and I were drinking coffee in the church narthex, talking about how our lawns and gardens had struggled to survive the drought conditions during that August. Wayne told me he didn't have a single weed in his lawn as a result. He said as he walked across his yard, he just pulled anything that was green!

I asked Wayne what there is about weeds—like crabgrass and dandelions—that enables them to withstand the lack of rain--unlike grass. He gave me a pretty logical explanation, which I have since forgotten, but which got me to thinking and doing some research about how plants are able to survive less-than-optimal conditions. Which ones do, and which ones don't—such as impatiens, which are like small children needing a drink of water every night before they go to bed? They need lots of TLC.

You have to admire weeds. They are survivors. One botanist said "Weeds survive under circumstances where our cultivated plants cannot stand up against nature's caprices. Weeds resist conditions, such as drought, acidity of soil, lack of humus and mineral deficiencies." I like that: *Weeds resist conditions.*

We know that weeds are any undesirable members of the plant kingdom. Some people define weeds as an unwanted and useless plant. If we were more generous, we might define them as plants that are only unwanted in a particular place. The term *weed* in its general sense is a subjective one; a number of "weeds" have been used in gardens. For example, the corncockle was a common field weed exported from Europe along with wheat, but is now sometimes grown as a garden plant. Some modern species of valued flowers actually originated as weeds and have been bred by people into garden plants for their flowers or foliage.

Eeyore, in *Winnie-the-Pooh*, said "Weeds are flowers, too, once you get to know them."[1] Maybe that's another reason I'm fond of weeds. I'd like to think that I become more desirable, at least tolerable, the more you get to know me. A plant species can only be called a weed if humans have not yet found a use for it. I'm trusting that someday my virtues will become more obvious. My preaching professor in seminary, George Buttrick, used to tell of the time a man tried to purge his garden of thistles by digging them up. One day he saw a whole hillside filled with thistles and began to weep; he was never going to be able to rid the world of thistles. The next Sunday, to his surprise, when he arrived at church, he found a woman arranging the altar flowers: they were Scotch thistles, and they were beautiful.[2] Whole fields of some weeds can be absolutely breathtaking.

Weeds are anything but fragile. But in general, they are pesky and troublesome. They compete with our desired plants for space, soil, nutrients, moisture and sunlight. Some weeds are a nuisance because they have thorns or prickles, some have chemicals that cause skin irritation or are hazardous if eaten or have parts that come off and attach to fur or clothes.

As much as we hate them, you have to admire them. They seem to

[1] Attributed to A. A. Milne

[2] George A Buttrick, *God Pain and Evil*, (Nashville: Abingdon Press, 1966), 44.

have a faster growth rate that enables them to outpace desirable plants. They are the first to grow up, flower and set seeds, ensuring that there will be subsequent generations of their species. Perennial weeds often have underground stems that spread out under the soil surface or, like ground ivy, have creeping stems that root and spread out over the ground. Some of them even secrete toxins into the soil to deter other plants from germinating.

They adapt to adverse conditions. Many of them have seeds that remain viable in the soil for many years. They are opportunistic. They spread their stems and leaves to catch more sunlight. As we've seen during times of drought, they are capable of resisting dry conditions. They know how to go dormant until conditions improve. They can contract their roots and slow their growth during extremely dry periods. They respond quickly to whatever moisture or nutrients are available to them. In a drought, weeds grow thicker cuticles, a waxy covering that prevents moisture loss and serves as a barrier to herbicide absorption. Weeds also have thick, tough stems and deep root systems that compete with the crop for limited moisture. And in extreme heat, which often accompanies drought, weed leaves roll up to minimize moisture loss and surface area.

That's why I'd rather be a weed. It's not that I want to feel unwanted. I just want to be a survivor. I want to be able to overcome whatever life throws at me. There's nothing much good that can be said about crabgrass, except that it survives. No matter what the conditions are or where its seeds take it.

You'll remember what Robert Fulghum said about the dandelions in his yard. A similar statement was made by the essayist Samuel Pickering, Jr., writing in the *New York Times,* "No other flower embodies the American spirit as well as the dandelion…Neither the strong winds nor heavy rains can break the dandelion. When the petals of the dogwood blossoms are scattered and the peony is beaten to the ground, the dandelion still holds its head up bravely."

Too many people are waiting for a more opportune time in life and looking for a more desirable place. I'd advise: "Flourish where you are." "Hang on." "Survive until you thrive."

I recently read of a young girl who graduated from a high school in South Carolina. When she was 18 months old, her father killed her mother and then shot himself. Her aunt was granted custody, but she was on drugs. Child Support Services took her away and she was finally placed with another relative. When she graduated, she told a reporter "I've learned to focus on my potential and not my limitations." She was given a scholarship to attend college.

Twenty years before J. K. Rowling became the billionaire author of the Harry Potter books, she was a single mother on welfare who was having a hard time finding enough money for bus fare.

The woman whom some say is the most influential woman in the world, Oprah Winfrey, was born to unwed impoverished teenagers in the backwoods of Mississippi. She was abused by male relatives and became pregnant at age fourteen. She determined that those devastating circumstances would not determine her future.

I recently read an obituary that inspired me. A young man, 27 years old, died in a neighboring city. He was on a national champion Quiz Bowl team in High School. He played in two orchestras. He was awarded a National Merit Scholarship and graduated with honors. He attended Indiana University on a full academic scholarship. He graduated with distinction, admitted to Phi Beta Kappa. He entered Medical School and completed his first year. During that time, he went through his *fifth* surgery. He had been diagnosed with a brain tumor his last year of High School. Remarkable perseverance against a horrible disease. It never slowed him down or stopped him.

What can you do where you are, under your current conditions, in your present situation? Mario Gomez was 63 years old. He had been mining in Chile since he was 12. On August 5, 2010, while he was working 2,300 feet below the surface, and about three miles from the mine entrance, a cave-in occurred. One group was working near the entrance and escaped immediately. But a group of 33 men was deep inside and trapped by the rock fall. They tried to escape through a ventilation shaft system, but the ladders required by mining safety codes were missing. Mario Gomez was the oldest miner. He became the religious leader. He requested statuettes of saints and a crucifix so the men could construct a shrine inside the mine. The Vatican provided 33 mini-Bibles and 33 rosaries. They held Bible studies. They sang hymns. He began counseling the miners, aiding the efforts of surface psychologists. Surrounded by 700,000 tons of rock. That reminds me of what we read in the book of Acts about Paul's time in the Philippian prison. They put him in the innermost cell and fastened his feet in the stocks. But a verse says, "About midnight Paul and Silas were praying and singing hymns to God, and the prisoners were listening to them" (Acts 16:25).

Can you have church while trapped a half-mile underground, or chained in a prison? Isn't there always a reason to praise God whatever your circumstance or situation?

There's one other thing I want to say about weeds. They generally produce more seeds than more desirable plants. A single crabgrass plant may produce up to 150,000 seeds. It is more prolific than other weeds because it is able to produce seeds below the typical mowing depth of most lawn mowers. In fact, the whirling blade of the mower only encourages seed dispersion.

You'll remember Jesus told parables about sowing seeds. He compared his words, the good news of the Kingdom of God, to seeds.

I read something a teacher wrote about how words are like seeds. She said that the words we speak sow seeds in the minds of those who hear. The formed word is like the shell of the seed. "It passes swiftly in conversation: just a couple of syllables, spoken and then gone. And yet, like the seed in the earth, the word may have vanished from view, but there, under the surface, it enters a transformational process." Some sprout into beneficial experiences in the lives of those who are listening. Some offer encouragement or inspiration. A proverb reminds us that "a good word cheers up the human heart" (Prov 12:25). The teacher added, "you must look inside yourself at every utterance to know what kinds of seeds you are tossing to the wind" and "make your sowing of words more intentional."

Ralph Waldo Emerson said, "The creation of a thousand forests is in one acorn." There is an anonymous saying that "A person who sows seeds of kindness enjoys a perpetual harvest." Paul wrote to the Galatians that whatever we sow, we shall reap. That's true of our words. And it's a fact of nature that seeds produce after their own kind. Something we say can take root and change how other people feel about themselves or their situation. You see, it's okay to think small sometimes. Planting tiny seeds in a small space can change the whole world. In one of those parables Jesus taught, he said that when seeds fall on good soil, they bring forth grain, some a hundredfold. I can only wonder what opportunities were missed because of words I never spoke. Simple words can be powerful, like "Hang on." "You can do it." "It's going to be alright." "I love you." "I'm praying for you."

Isn't it time others heard that? Is it time we started to sow the seeds of God's goodness and grace?

Questions for Contemplating and Conversing

1. How do you feel about weeds?
2. Do you spend a lot of time and money eradicating weeds?
3. Do you have neighbors who ignore the dandelions and crabgrass in their lawns? How do you feel about that?
4. What gives you the strength to persevere through life's difficulties?
5. In what ways are you flexible, persistent, able to overcome undesirable conditions?
6. What is the main lesson you learned from this chapter?

14. Blooming Where You Are Planted

"Happiness, not in another place but this place…not for another hour, but this hour."
–Walt Whitman

Several years ago, John Steinbeck wrote a book that chronicled a 10,000-mile trip he took across America with his dog, Charley. He began his journey with a conversation he had with a fellow in Connecticut. The man was admiring Steinbeck's custom-built motor home. He said,

"You going in that?"
"Sure."
"Where?"
"All over."
"And then," Steinbeck writes, "I saw what I was to see so many times on the journey—a look of longing."
"Gee! I wish I could go," said the man.
"Don't you like it here?"
"Sure, it's all right. But I wish I could go."
"You don't even know where I'm going."

"I don't care. I'd like to go anywhere."[1]

Have you ever felt like that and said, "I don't care where, I'd just like to go somewhere else. I'd like to be anywhere but here"?

Throughout my ministry, I've listened to people talk about their restlessness and discontent, pining for, planning for a different job, changing their family situation, relocating, changing neighborhoods, or leaving one church for another. Wanting a change of scenery, their dreams are expressed with an "if only..." "If only I were married to someone else." "If only I had a different job." "If only I had better people to work with." "If only I lived in a better house." I could relate to them, because preachers aren't immune from that. Many are always thinking they could be more successful anywhere else than where they happen to be. They are always looking for "greener pastorates."

Just as we may wait for a more opportune time, we may look for a more desirable place.

Whether in selecting some plants from the seed catalogue or when setting them out in the garden, there is one kind of flower I like the best. It's the one that is described in seed catalogues as "Suitable for shade or sun. Does not need rich soil. Can stand neglect. Will thrive anywhere." The reason I like them so much is that there are lots of other flowers which require a certain temperature, exact conditions, the right amount of sun, and rich soil in order to flourish. They take a lot of extra care and pampering to get them to bloom. Gardeners call them "temperamental." Do you know any people like that? I think we call them "high maintenance."

Additionally, I also like the kinds of plants that withstand transplanting. Whenever I move from one house to another, I try to take some of my flowers with me. It's been interesting to see the difference between those that didn't mind the move, and those who continue to protest. Some, like St. Paul, (and dandelions), seem content wherever they end up--those "anywhere will do" people. No matter what the conditions, whether favorable or favorable, they blossom and bloom—not like the people who demand perfect conditions in order for them to feel they can grow, bloom, or bear fruit. Do you know any people like that? They don't just survive; they thrive, regardless of where they are.

I guess Paul was one of those. He wrote to his friends in Philippi,

[1] John Steinbeck, *Travels with Charley*, (Japan: Penguin Books, 1997), 21-22

"I have learned to be content with whatever I have…In any and all circumstances I have learned the secret of being well-fed and of going hungry, of having plenty and of being in need." (Phil 4:11-12). Obviously, Paul was able to bloom wherever he was planted. I guess you could compare Paul to a dandelion. You never hear a dandelion sit in the crack of the driveway complaining, "I wish I were somewhere else. Then I could bloom and produce ten zillion seeds." No, they just grow wherever they are. (And produce ten zillion seeds.) I can hear Jesus telling a parable about dandelions, can't you? He might have made the point that we should make the most of any situation in which we find ourselves. "Bloom where you are planted" sounds like something Jesus might have said, doesn't it?

If there was a Bible passage to put on a plaque in a patch of weeds it would be from Paul: *I am okay with being anywhere, in any and all circumstances.*

The truth is, there is always the lure of those faraway places which seem to promise a more exciting time for us. That's why Jesus told a story about the prodigal son who "gathered all he had and took his journey into a far country." Maybe he had become bored back on the farm. Whatever the reason, he decided to pull up roots and set out for the "far country" where he believed things would be better for him. Someone should have recited an old poem to him that warns:

I wish I had a ticket for Siam.
I'm getting pretty bored with where I am.
But when I'm in Siam why all I'll do
Is wish I had a ticket for Peru.

Someone should have reminded the young son that the problem is not be where you are that's boring--*you* may be boring. And wherever you go, you will meet yourself. Ralph Waldo Emerson said that traveling is foolish and that place is nothing. We may believe we can lose our sadness by going to some other place, but when we wake up in that new location, Emerson cautioned, "there beside me is the stern face—the sad self, unrelenting, identical—that I fled from." Many of us seek what has been called "the geographical cure" for everything that bothers us. We believe changing locations will change our lives. Otherwise, why are we always so much on the road, going from place to place, wanting a "change of scenery"?

Place is nothing, Emerson said. The only cure for someplace else is meanwhile, here and now-- nevertheless. Humorist Will Rogers used to say that when he grew tired of the same old surroundings and would wish for a new place to live and work, he would pick another city that sounded attractive. Before he pulled up stakes and moved there, though, he would subscribe to the leading newspaper in his proposed new home and read that paper for thirty days. Rogers said that he would always decide not to move. The news from where he planned to be was no better than the news where he already was.

I've thought about writing a book for ministers to hand out when they are being moved to another congregation. I'd title it *Changing Churches or Changing Churches?* You may have to think about that for a time. One way out of a difficult appointment is to change churches. Move on. But another is to find ways of changing the church where we have committed ourselves to stay. Now that I've written that, I guess there should be a better option: changing our attitudes and changing ourselves.

The most natural response to a tough situation is for us to walk away. A 75-year-old man went to his doctor for a physical. The doctor was amazed that he didn't find a single thing wrong with him. Then he said, "You really have the body of a man 25 years younger. What's your secret?" The man explained, "Well, when my wife and I were married 50 years ago, we made an agreement. We decided that we would never quarrel. When we have a difference of opinion that is potentially explosive, and we see a fight is coming on, she just stays in the house, and I go out for a long walk. I guess my good health is due to the fact that for 50 years, I've pretty much lived an outdoor life."

When it comes to a tough situation, isn't the question to ask, "*what* can I get out if it?" rather than "*how* can I get out of it?"

I once read of a fellow who decided to sell his home and buy another, so he wrote out an ad which described in detail what kind of house he wanted. When he had finished, he realized it sounded a whole lot like the house he was already living in. He just hadn't looked at it closely enough.

There's a great old story that you may have heard. Russell Conwell, the founder of Temple University, used the money he made from giving the same speech over six thousand times to endow the university. His speech was turned into a book, *Acres of Diamonds*. It's a story he says he learned from an old Arab guide in the Middle East on one of his trips there. A certain Ali Hafed owned a very large farm, with orchards, grain fields and gardens. He was wealthy and contented, but he always wanted to own the largest diamond in the world. If he had that one diamond the size of his thumb, he knew he could purchase more farms and fields, and if he were so fortunate to discover a diamond mine, he would be guaranteed all the wealth he would ever want. He decided he'd go off and find that diamond mine. He learned that there was such a mine, near a river that runs through white sands, between high mountains *somewhere*. So he sold his farm, collected his money, left his family, and away he went to search for a river with white sands, between high mountains. Ali Hafed wandered about Palestine, then went to Europe, and finally his money was all gone and he was in rags and poverty, and he stood on the ocean's shore in Spain, tempted to throw himself into the sea.

Meanwhile, one day "back on the farm," the man who had purchased Ali's farm was leading his camel back into one of the gardens to get a drink, and as that camel put its nose into the shallow water of the garden brook, the man noticed a curious flash of light from the white sands of the stream. He pulled out a pebble, put it in his pocket, took it into the house and put in on the mantel, but soon forgot about it. Sometime later, a friend came in and saw the stone and exclaimed, "A diamond! Has Ali Hafed returned?" "Oh, no, Ali Hafed has not returned, and this is not a diamond. That's nothing but a stone we found right out here in our own garden." Finally, his friend convinced the owner that it was a diamond, so the two of them rushed out into the garden and began to dig in the white sand. As they came across other more beautiful gems than the first one, they stopped and looked around them at the high mountains that rose above them. They had discovered the most magnificent diamond mine in the entire world.

The Arab who told Conwell that story concluded: "Had Ali Hafed remained at home and dug in his own cellar, or underneath his own wheat fields, or in his own garden, instead of wretchedness, starvation and death in a strange land, he would have had acres of diamonds."

Dig for diamonds where you are. Bloom where you are planted. Find contentment no matter what your circumstance. You may be surrounded by diamonds in the rough. You may have to dig deeper to discover what you've been looking for. Henry Comstock laid claim to a silver deposit in Nevada in 1859. It never lived up to his hopes and dreams for a rich find. Before long, he was offered $11,000 for it and sold it. He sold out too soon. The Comstock mine proved to be the greatest silver deposit in history. Its new owners just dug a bit deeper and made $340,000,000 during the next thirty years.

For many years, Ernest Campbell was the pastor of New York City's famed Riverside Church. He wrote in one of his books about the time he did something he had wanted to do for a long time. He said he became a "tourist in his own hometown." What if we took some time off to stay in our towns or cities, pretending we were first-time visitors? (I'll confess that I've spent nearly half of my life in or near Indianapolis—and I have never been to the Indianapolis Motor Speedway Museum.)

It is a matter of looking around and appreciating what we have right where we are.

Why not try that? Be a tourist in your home today. Or at work tomorrow. Enjoy what you have where you are. Try to look with fresh eyes at what may have grown too familiar to you.

I suspect that for all of us, there are some unexplored areas just waiting for you to spend time looking for "diamonds." I was once given a little devotional entitled *South Forty.* Farmers often refer to unproductive acreage as the "south forty," or "back forty." It's a neglected area that with proper cultivation can prove very productive, but it takes hard work. The devotional writer suggests that there are parts of our lives that have been neglected, but which might be productive if they were plowed and cultivated.

Where's your back forty?

The great architect Frank Lloyd Wright liked to say that the secret of real creativity in every area of life lay in its limitations. When you are severely limited and have to work and live in a constricted and restricted area, your inner creativity is most challenged and you are more likely to produce your greatest work.

We can illustrate that. Elias Howe was poor, both in health and in finances. He would watch his wife painfully plying her sewing needle in order that she might earn enough money for their next meal. He thought there should be a way to save her and the other women from such tedious work. So, in six months, he invented the sewing machine.

Alexander Graham Bell was a teacher in a school for the deaf. He fell in love with one of his pupils, married her, and in order to help her overcome her handicap he set out to develop a hearing apparatus for her. In the process of experimentation, he invented the telephone.

They did not choose to complain or to opt out of their situations. They simply changed the focus of their attention to the needs of others.

Nobody should ever consider themselves a victim of circumstances. Put a man behind prison bars and you get a John Bunyan. Bury him in the snows of Valley Forge and get a George Washington. Have him born in abject poverty and you get an Abraham Lincoln. Fanny Crosby wrote our most beloved gospel hymns, and she was blind. Beethoven was deaf.

Paul wrote some of our most beloved passages of scripture while in chains, awaiting death. He never used that as an excuse for not being able to do his job, which was to convert persons to Jesus Christ. We noted how Paul had written of his contentment regardless of his place. He wrote that to the Philippians. It was in Philippi that he had freed a slave girl from her owners, and that got him and his companion, Silas, beaten and thrown into jail for disturbing the city. There they sat, bound—but also determined to make the most of an awful situation. They were miraculously provided with an escape, but not before they converted the man who had guarded them. And not just him, but his entire family was baptized, and believed.

Don't use the place where you are planted as an excuse. In 1910, two men wearing caps and gowns stood in an academic procession at Columbia University where they were to receive honorary degrees. When they introduced themselves, one said, "My name is Mayo, and I am a doctor in a little Minnesota town." Jesus lived in a remote corner of the world. He lived only thirty-three years, never traveling more than a hundred and fifty miles from the place where he was born. His homeland was, and is, one of the most troubled places on earth. He had all sorts of excuses for not doing much of anything with his life. But he stayed where he had been placed, put down his roots, and no one else has ever done more with his life than he did.

Someone has said, "Life is not someday or somewhere else—but meanwhile back at the ranch." Sometime ago there was an article about that great scientist, George Washington Carver, entitled *No Greener Pastures*. His philosophy was quoted as being "Start where you are, with what you have; and make something of it." That's how he could change the eroded soil fields and red clay hills of the south into green and growing pastures.

Many years ago, I clipped a column from "Dear Abby." It was about life's detours. But it concluded with a powerful witness from the mother of a special-needs child. A part of what she wrote:

> I am often asked to describe the experience of raising a child with a disability—to try to help people who have not shared that unique experience to understand it, to imagine how it would feel. It's like this...When you're going to have a baby, it's like

planning a fabulous vacation trip—to Italy. You buy a bunch of guidebooks and make your wonderful plans…After months of eager anticipation, the day finally arrives. You pack your bags and off you go. Several hours later, the plane lands. The stewardess comes in and says, "Welcome to Holland." "Holland?" you say. "What do you mean, Holland? I signed up for Italy! I'm supposed to be in Italy. All my life I've dreamed of going to Italy!" But there's been a change in the flight plan. They've landed in Holland and there you must stay…So you must go out and buy new guidebooks. And you must learn a whole new language. And you will meet a whole new group of people you would never have met. It's just a different place. It's slower paced than Italy, less flashy than Italy. But, after you've been there for a while and you catch your breath, you look around, and you begin to notice that Holland has windmills. Holland has tulips. Holland even has Rembrandts…If you spend your life mourning the fact that you didn't get to Italy, you may never be free to enjoy the very special, the very lovely things about Holland.

Questions for Contemplating and Conversing

1. Why would you like to be somewhere other than where you are right now?
2. Have you ever moved away in an effort to make your life better?
3. Are you more of a "how can I get out of it?" or a "what can I get out of it?" person?
4. In what areas of your life have you looked for *greener pastures?* House? Job? Partner?
5. Can you list ten things that make you glad you are where you are?
6. What is the main lesson you learned from this chapter?

15. When the Rabbits Eat Your Lettuce

"The art of being wise is the art of knowing what to overlook."
-William James

One of my churches had a rather unique sanctuary. It wasn't the fact we used chairs and not pews, or that it was a nearly round room. No, it was the doors. There must have been a dozen or more of them, leading from the sanctuary into my office, classrooms, the library, the choir room, the kitchen, and outdoors. The congregation was used to the informality of the setting and that was the style of worship, and yet, the number of folks going in and out of those doors during worship was both a horrible distraction and a constant disruption. I never felt we could maintain an atmosphere which enabled us to sense the presence of God.

I never felt comfortable leading worship and preaching in that setting.

In the same way, when we come into the garden, there are "disruptions" of all kinds that seem to work against what we are there for and rob of us what we want.

There is a passage from a rather obscure book of the Old Testament—which is really a collection of love poems. (Some parts might be labeled PG-13.) The book also includes many references to the beauty of the natural world, including this poem written in the springtime:

> My beloved speaks and says to me:
> "Arise, my love, my fair one,
> and come away;
> for now, the winter is past,
> the rain is over and gone.
> The flowers appear on the earth;
> the time of singing has come,
> and the voice of the turtle-dove
> is heard in our land.
> The fig tree puts forth its figs,
> and the vines are in blossom;
> they give forth fragrance.
> Arise, my love, my fair one,
> and come away
> O my dove, in the clefts of the rock,
> in the covert of the cliff,
> let me see your face,
> let me hear your voice;
> for your voice is sweet,
> and your face is lovely.
> Catch us the foxes,
> the little foxes,
> that ruin the vineyards
> for our vineyards are in blossom." (Song 2: 10 – 15)

A vegetable garden has been described by one cynic as "One of a vast number of free outdoor restaurants operated by charity-minded amateurs to provide healthful, balanced meals for all the insects, birds and animals in the neighborhood." Then there is this definition of a fruit: "A general term for the seed-bearing part of a plant that is eaten by birds or worms, drops off, rots, gets funny-looking spots on it, isn't what was pictured in the catalog or doesn't appear on the plant at all." When that happens to our garden, we shoulder our squirt-bottles filled with chemicals just like our ancestors shouldered their muskets.

I can especially relate to that definition of a vegetable garden being a free restaurant providing balanced meals for birds and animals. Back when I had a fairly large vegetable garden, the rabbits would line up waiting to get at my lettuce like a line of cars going through the drive-through at McDonald's. I tried everything to discourage them, so much so that my garden looked like a flea market. I placed pie tins tied to stakes, human hair, dried blood, fake snakes, real snakes, a dog, tapes of my sermons playing loudly, and pictures of Ozzy Osbourne. I heard of, but never tried, sprinkling baby powder near the plants.

One of my friends told me the only solution is just planting enough stuff for our family <u>and</u> for all the animals. I'm not sure I'm ready for that kind of generous gesture on my part since I've never gotten over something that happened when we lived on the south side of Indianapolis. I had a fence around my garden because the Rabbit Restaurant Review had given my lettuce five stars that year. One day I was going out to hoe when I heard a rustling near one of the rows. A family of rabbits had built their nest in the ground on the *inside* of the elaborate barricade I had constructed. That struck me as a kind of "in-your-face" act of contempt, so ever since it's been war--a war that I know I cannot win. The enemy is far too smart. My sister was having a problem with raccoons eating her sweet corn. I told her I read that, to a raccoon, "six feet of wire fence is merely a jungle gym upon which it can work up an appetite before raiding the corn."

Which is a roundabout way of getting to my point. I don't know if they had rabbits in Biblical times, but they had foxes. There is that line from the Song of Solomon that seems to have no relation to any of the rest of the romantic poetry or to the rest of the book. "Catch us the foxes, the little foxes, that ruin the vineyards--for our vineyards are in blossom." Just as that love song is interrupted by advice about the little foxes, so our plans are often interrupted, and it is the "little foxes" that do it.

Or in our day, it's the cute little rabbits, or chipmunks, or squirrels. Once, I remember, it was the goldfinches. When we lived in Rushville, I put a basketball goal on our garage roof. I had wanted my son to have a chance to hit some of his shots, so it was about eight feet off the ground--not the usual ten feet. My mistake became obvious when some of Bill's older and taller friends began "slam-dunking" the ball and hanging on the net. It wasn't long before we began to notice the fibers of the cloth net were quickly disintegrating. I accused the neighborhood young folks of pulling on it and ripping it down and asked them not to do it. They denied ever having done that. One day I discovered the real cause of the net being pulled apart. The culprit was not some 150-pound kid. It was a tiny goldfinch! I happened on that beautiful little bird, one of the dozens who lived in and around our yard, perched on the rim tugging and pulling at the cloth net to be used as material for his nest! Fascinated with his ingenuity and creative approach to nest building, I let him finish his job and then replaced the net.

That's a parable of life. Oftentimes it is not the big, heavyweight problems that destroy our plans and purposes, it's the little things. Trifles, interruptions, disappointments, frustrations, irritations, and little annoyances. Little foxes eating the vines. Rabbits eating your lettuce. Some of us never scale the mountains because we are too busy with the molehills. We need to become more aware of the potential bigness of the little, how we major in minors.

Sometimes it's not anything even as big as rabbits. Just insects. For more than four centuries a great tree stood on the slope of Long's Peak, in Colorado, withstanding lightning, avalanches and windstorms. Finally, it was destroyed by an army of tiny beetles--insects so small that they could be crushed between your forefinger and thumb. They ate their way through the bark and gradually destroyed the inner strength of the tree. Sometimes we can withstand the bigger attacks better than the little ones.

We are so consumed and eaten-up by a lot of little things. We may envy the fellow in New York City who applied for a job as a horseshoer for the police department's horses. He said, "I might have been a doctor, lawyer, teacher, but I drive a truck in Brooklyn. I don't like driving a truck. There are too many nuts on the road. With horseshoeing, there's just me and the horse." Sometimes life gets to be too much for us. We wish we could just say, "If there's just me and the horse, I could get along." There are times when I said to myself, "If I could just spend twenty hours a week working on sermons and another twenty looking after people's needs, I'd feel a lot better about this job." But sermon preparation gets shoved to the side. It was hard to use my office at the church for a "study." There are too many interruptions. So many little things. "Administrivia," as one minister calls it. Usually, I just went to the church in the morning, put my mind in neutral and went where I was pushed the rest of the day. I had to ask myself, "What is it I came here to do?" Most days we end up chasing rabbits rather than staying on the main trail.

Seldom do we march straight toward our goal. There are so many distractions, detours and things that detain us. In some cities, fire trucks are being equipped with an invention that will turn all of the traffic lights green as an emergency vehicle approaches an intersection. Wouldn't it be wonderful if you had nothing but green lights all along your journey through life? I know of nothing that can do that for us. Life is filled with stops and starts. It is unrealistic to believe it can ever be otherwise.

I've learned from gardening that most insects and diseases attack plants that are otherwise "under stress" from drought or some other undesirable condition. I think we are more susceptible to attack when we are stressed-out. Self-care is essential.

It isn't easy to do that. We allow ourselves so little down-time. With all the gadgets and so-called "labor saving devices" technology is offering us these days, that probably means there are just more things to go wrong and more ways we can be interrupted. Did you see the cartoon titled "A 90's Vacation" which showed a family sitting on the beach? The mother is on a cellular phone saying, "Can you hold on? Someone's on call waiting." The father holds a lap top computer saying to himself, "I better check my e-mail." One son calls out, "Mom, your fax is coming in." Another son says, "Oops. There goes my beeper," and the daughter, "It's time I checked my voice mail," as she held a phone to her ear. Is it any wonder we are being consumed by so many interruptions, having made ourselves so available and accessible? Is there any way we can survive?

Let me offer a few suggestions on how we might. One is to stop worrying about what you can't control. The other is the title of Richard Carlson's popular book, *Don't Sweat the Small Stuff and It's All Small Stuff.*

Interestingly, learning what we can ignore leads to the subject of perfectionism. We already know that perfectionism is bad for our health, a major contributor to depression, high blood pressure, chronic indigestion, ulcers and migraine headaches. Perfectionists are too demanding and overly critical. They try to meet impossible standards placed on themselves and others. They are seldom satisfied.

Because perfectionists have set a standard of "no less than the best," anything that keeps them from realizing a score of 100 can be disastrous. Because the world is imperfect, they have set themselves up for a losing battle. The focus on what's wrong fosters a feeling of discontent and dissatisfaction. It's a given that perfectionists see life as something to be fixed--or rather long lists of what needs to be fixed. Disorganized closets, scratches on the car, the way someone behaves or lives their life--all that and more can contribute to disastrous days.

There is some good advice for dealing with that. One simple reminder is to do as I was advised about planting enough lettuce for my family and for Peter Rabbit's family. Make allowances for interruptions. Write into each day's schedule time when your plans will change. Prioritize being flexible over rigidity. Expect that a certain percentage of your plans are going to change. Make allowances for the inevitable and cross them off when they occur.

Charles Darwin discovered an extraordinary thing in one of his voyages in the Pacific Ocean. He found an unusual type of seaweed. It floated on the waves, was tossed by wind and tide, and sometimes flung itself violently against the rocks along the coast. Still, it lived on while other forms of animal and vegetable life perished. Rocks were being pulverized into powder under the force of the waves, but not that sea weed. Darwin entered in his notebook: "I know of few things more surprising than to see this plant growing and flourishing amid those great breakers of the western ocean which no mass of rock, be it ever so hard, can long resist." The secret of this plant's endurance was its flexibility, its inner strength. We need to bend a little. Go with the flow.

Remind yourself that no matter what, life is okay the way it is. The purpose of life isn't to get everything done, to cross items off a list, to empty your in-basket, to reach all your goals--but to enjoy each step along the way. Someone has said that when you die, there will still be unfinished business to take care of and someone else will do it for you. Another helpful hint is to say, "I'm not OK, but it's OK." To develop a philosophy of "good-enough" or "adequate." One woman created a list of what "adequate" meant to her:

> Adequate means I will not fall apart when an unexpected guest walks into my uncleaned house.
> Adequate means the world doesn't stand or fall by my accomplishments or failures.
> Adequate means sometimes my children will be wonderful, and sometimes they will be terrible, and that is OK.
> Adequate means I can like other people and enjoy them and accept them even if they are not perfect.
> Adequate means that comparing myself to others is not going to tell me anything worthwhile.
> Adequate means being able to say, "I am sorry" and then letting go.
> Adequate means not being responsible for everyone else.

Adopting an attitude that says *adequate is good enough* can also enable us to feel more forgiven than driven. That's why we should not just pray,

"Lord, forgive me for not being perfect," but also "Lord, forgive me for wanting to be God."

The second kind of person most susceptible to being eaten by the little things of life is the "catastrophizer." They blow things out of proportion. They believe everything really is a very big deal. Not everything is an emergency. It has been suggested that catastrophizers might ask themselves, "Aren't you really being only annoyed rather than tortured; isn't what you are experiencing a sad event rather than a tragic event; can't you live through the frustration without it killing you?"

Many of the irritations in life aren't nearly as important as we believe they are. Arguments, mistakes, frustrations may simply be irrelevant in the grand sweep of history. I had a secretary in one church who would suggest we give challenges and conflicts "the Ten-Year Rule." In ten years, will we even remember this? T. S. Eliot has prayed, "Teach us to care and not to care."[1] I think that means we need help understanding what not to care about. Maybe the best way to deal with the rabbits is to simply ignore them.

Even worse are those theatrical people who turn everything into a soap opera, making a big deal out of little things. They forget life isn't as bad as they're making it out to be. In a soap opera, characters take little things so seriously that everything someone else does seems to offend them and they end up talking to others about how awful it is. When that happens in a church, disagreements escalate into dividing into good guys vs. bad guys, and we spend more energy worrying about getting our way than trying to determine God's way.

Finally, as Beethoven said, "A few fly bites cannot stop a spirited horse." Maybe we need to put blinders on, stay focused on our goals and task and destination. Those who are so easily distracted and detoured probably don't know where they are headed, anyway. There is a little cemetery in the shadows of the Matterhorn, that mountain on the frontier between Italy and Switzerland which stretches almost 15,000 feet into the sky. In that cemetery, there is a grave marker with these words: "We who lie here scorned the lesser peaks." Some people are at the mercy of every challenge and forego the greater adventures. We need to scorn the lesser peaks… and piques.

I've often thought life is a lot like registering for classes in college. We usually declare our major and then take the required courses in that area.

[1] T. S. Eliot, "Ash-Wednesday," in *T. S. Eliot: Collected Poems*, 1909-1962, (New York: Harcourt Brace & Company, 1991), 86.

We don't take every course that's offered. We just can't afford the time and energy to do that. If you haven't yet "declared the major of your life," or determined what it is you are here to accomplish, maybe it's time to do that.

What is your personal mission statement? What is the area you are majoring in? Do all the things you spend your time doing every day bring you closer to fulfilling the requirements?

What's important to you? Would you learn how to answer that if we checked your checking account? Your calendar? What are your priorities in life?

Questions for Contemplating and Conversing

1. What irritates you that from another perspective just might be a minor inconvenience?
2. Would you say you make mountains out of molehills? When do you do that?
3. Are there ways you might consider yourself a *perfectionist?*
4. Are you able to convince yourself that sometimes *adequate* is good enough?
5. Are you a person who believes everything should go your way all the time?
6. How do you feel about people who are catastrophizers?
7. What is the main lesson you learned from this chapter?

16. Looking Through Seed Catalogues

"Don't judge each day by the harvest you reap but by the seeds that you plant."

-Robert Louis Stevenson

Do you remember when we used to call the Sears Roebuck, J. C. Penney, and Montgomery Ward catalogues "Wish Books"? That's pretty much what they were, books that had just about everything we ever wished for or wanted to make our lives better. I can remember circling a football outfit in the Sears catalogue. I wasn't very athletic, so I thought having the outfit might change that. At least I'd look the part! My folks made a deal with me. If I practiced the piano a half hour a day, I would eventually accumulate enough "points" that they would order the outfit.

I never wore a football jersey or shoulder pads. I am sure there were lots of other things I did get, but I still remember what I didn't get. Now that I'm grown up, and we don't get those big catalogues through the mail anymore, I have another version of a "wish book." It's called a seed catalogue, and I get dozens of them. They are probably the best things I know of to help us make it through the days of winter. Sometimes it's as overwhelming to decide which seeds or plants to order as I remember it was when my folks would give me a quarter and let me walk around the toy counters at Kresge's. It would take me hours to decide.

Seed catalogues have come to represent something even more important to me. They parallel what happens in life. The first thing they teach us is that you have to plan—as well as plant—ahead. There's a great quote that says, "All of the flowers of all our tomorrows are in the seeds of today." There's something about all those marvelous pictures of flowers and fruits in the seed catalogues that motivate us to order the seeds and to try to come up with what is pictured. Seldom do we have our goals and end-results pictured so clearly. We are taught to "begin with the end in mind," because if you can "conceive it you can achieve it." It's that way with our marriages: What do you want to be doing and feeling on your fiftieth wedding anniversary? What memories do you want to have? What do you need to do today to make these into what will someday be called "the good old days"? It's that way with our children. What kind of adult citizens and Christian men and women do you want them to turn out to be? How we answer that goes a long way in determining what we do with them today.

I have a friend who encouraged me to start this new year with a "wish list." She wrote in an e-mail: "New Year's Day is a good self-inventory day. What did I learn? And what am I hoping to do in the new year? Use the energy from painful experiences to move you forward. Write 'I wish" at the beginning of every other line on an 8 ½ by 11-inch lined page. Take a deep breath and then write to fill in the lines until you have completed the page. It can be anything. Then go back and pick out a couple of your responses. Think of what you can do to take a baby-step toward doing or having whatever you wish for." I tried to do that this year. I failed.

Seed catalogues represent for me the hopes and dreams I have for my life. There's no catalogue for weeds, or brambles and briars. Just beautiful flowers and scrumptious fruits and vegetables. That's what we want for our lives, isn't it?

I once heard someone say the best things in life are paid for in advance. The bad things we do are paid for afterwards. That means we are take what we want in life and be willing to pay for it. And work for it. Every flower and plant pictured in those catalogues has to begin with a seed. That has to be planted. And watered. And fertilized. And pampered. And protected. There are no instant gardens.

I hate winter, except for the fact that's when seed catalogues arrive in the mail. Like the old Sears catalogues, they can be a source of both dreams and disappointments. Reality doesn't always match the pictured promises. I always wondered how many tomatoes they had to sort through until they found one as beautiful, imperfection-free, and red as the ones for which they offer seed packets. Not every seed germinates. Seedlings die from over-watering or under-watering. Or damping-off disease. (One year a mouse in the basement devoured a tray of my seedlings.)

So much of life comes to us as a wish book, a catalogue of dreams. We want to look like what those handsome or slim models look like. Or be as successful as the executive is with his new-fangled technological tool. Or be as happy as the families that are gathered around the table eating Campbell's tomato soup. I think the world does a terrific job showing us our dreams—and a dreadful job of helping us deal with our disappointments.

The Bible is, in a sense, a wish book. It's all about dreams and promises and faith, hope and love, and heaven and the abundant life, but it's not just a catalogue of what we want in life. It also helps us deal with our unfulfilled dreams and our daily disappointments. One scripture reading is like reading from a seed catalogue. Paul wrote to the Galatian Christians, "You reap whatever you sow…So let us not grow weary in doing what is right, for we will reap at harvest-time, if we do not give up" (Gal 6:7-9).

That makes perfect sense, doesn't it? Order some petunia seeds, plant them, and up will come petunias. Order tomato seeds, plant them, and up will come tomatoes. We reap what we sow. There is, Paul said, a direct correlation between what we give and what we receive, what we do and what we can expect in return. There will be a time when we can reap what we have sown. That's pretty much the way it is in the garden or on the farm.

But I'm not so sure it always works that way in other areas of our lives. I want to digress just a bit. Let me tell you about one of my biggest complaints about television evangelists. If you've ever watched the Trinity Broadcasting Network, you know that the main message is "sow a faith promise seed" and "God will bless you, God will bring you health and wealth, and as an added bonus, God will even help get your loved ones off drugs and get them saved." Seems to me that's a lot like selling miracles, making God into a Holy Lottery. Send something to the preachers and God will give you a "hundred-fold return." If you watch enough of that stuff, I promise you that you'll hear quoted Malachi 3:8-12.

> Bring the full tithe into the storehouse, so that there may be food in my house, and thus put me to the test, says the Lord of hosts; see if I will not open the windows of heaven for you and pour down for you an overflowing blessing.

They probably add something from the story of Isaac in the book of Genesis:

> Isaac sowed seed in that land, and in the same year reaped a hundredfold. The Lord blessed him, and the man became rich; he prospered more and more until he became very wealthy. (Gen 26:12-13).

Therefore, their argument goes, if you sow your seed in our ministry, God will bless you and make you rich. You'll reap a hundredfold.

Yeah, right! I've given enough money to the church over my life that if it worked that way I ought to be retired and living in Cancun! What distresses me even more than the false promises and deception of the TV preachers is the fact that people believe them, send in their so-called "seed faith" and sit back to wait for God to pay off.

So, like our expectation that our garden will look like those on the pages of the seed catalogues, since they seldom do, we need help dealing with life's disappointments. Life does not always work out as we pictured it or planned for it. There are no guarantees in life. I've even tried pasting the pictures of the beautiful flowers right next to the trays where I planted my seeds to inspire them to be all that they should be. Even that doesn't work. One catalogue says they guarantee their products to "perform as advertised." Not in my experience.

Again, disappointment is so much a part of gardening. So is becoming disheartened. In Cardinal Woolsey's farewell address in Shakespeare's *Henry the Eighth*, the chief advisor to the king laments:

> This is the state of man: to-day he puts forth
> The tender leaves of hopes, to-morrow blossoms,
> And bears his blushing honors thick upon him;
> The third day comes a frost, a killing frost…

Some years it's a frost, other years it's a drought, and, all the time, insects, disease and weeds. A. B. Bragdon wrote "The Old Campus," in which he expressed the feelings many gardeners have in the fall:

> Alas, how scant the sheaves for all the trouble,
> The toil, the pain and the resolve sublime—
> A few full ears; the rest but weeds and stubble,
> And withered wildflowers plucked before their time.

Most seed catalogues carry this disclaimer: "In some instances, the item ordered may be substituted with a product of equal or greater value." I've often wondered if that's the way God answers some of our prayers. We want answers to our prayers to be quick and easy. A long time ago I decided I would rather go through the lengthy and tedious and sometimes frustrating process of starting my own plants from seed. I could have prayed, "God, please put some pretty flowers in my yard." God would have answered, "Bill, buy a packet of seeds."

There is a legendary miracle that Eddie Rickenbacker experienced during World War II. He was a hero in both World War I and World War II. In that second war, he and a crew of seven were flying over the Pacific when their plane went down. All of the men survived, crawled out of the plane, and climbed into life rafts. They floated for days on the rough waters of the Pacific. They fought the sun, and sharks, and hunger. Their food ran out by the third day. No food and no water, they were hundreds of miles from land and no one knew where they were. On the eighth day, Rickenbacker suddenly felt something land on the top of his cap. It was a seagull. He managed to grab it and wring its neck. He tore the feathers off, and he and his starving crew ate part of it and then they used the intestines for bait. They caught fish which gave them food and more bait. That cycle continued until they were found and rescued.

Eddie Rickenbacker lived about another 30 years after that, telling everyone about the miracle of a lifesaving seagull.

What about when the seagull doesn't come? A few years ago, Robert Wise published a book with the inviting title, *When There Is No Miracle: Finding Hope in Pain and Suffering.* I would guess more of us can relate to the times when the seagull doesn't come and when there is no miracle, than to the story of Eddie Rickenbacker.

No seagull comes when loved ones die, jobs are taken away, when doctor's tests come back worse than feared. (No one was more intensely prayed for than my mother, and yet she died of cancer at 59. There was no miracle.)

I guess why I still believe in the Church is that we aren't just in the business of telling you how to make a deal with God. We are in the business of helping you get through those times prayers go unanswered and life seems to owe you an *apology*.

That's the message of a scene in one of my favorite plays, *A Thousand Clowns*, by Herb Gardner. An eccentric, Murray, is talking to a social worker about his failure to get a job—which he was required to do as the guardian of a young boy, Nick, who lives with him: "Picture, if you will, me. I am walking on East Fifty-first Street an hour ago and I decide to construct and develop a really decorative, general—all-purpose apology. Not complicated, just the words 'I am sorry,' said with a little style." Sandra, the social worker, interrupts: "Sorry for what?"
Murray continues:

> "Anything. For being late, early, stupid, asleep, silly, alive…Well, y'know when you're walking down the street talking to yourself how sometimes you suddenly say a coupla words out loud? So, I said, 'I'm sorry,' and this fella, complete stranger, he looks up a second and says, 'That's all right, Mac,' and goes right on. He automatically forgave me. I communicated. Five o'clock rush-hour in midtown you could say, 'Sir, I believe you hair is on fire,' and they wouldn't hear you. So, I decided to test the whole thing out scientifically. I stayed right there on the corner of Fifty-first and Lex for a while, just saying 'I'm sorry' to everybody that went by…Of course, some people just gave me a funny look, but Sandy I swear, seventy-five percent of them FORGAVE me…Oh, Sandy, it was fabulous. I had tapped some vast reservoir. Something had happened to all of them for which they felt SOMEbody should apologize…Sandy, I could run up on the roof right now and holler, 'I am sorry,' and a million people would holler right back, 'That's O. K., just see that you don't do it again!"

Murray then goes on to apologize to the social worker for not having gotten a job, as he promised her he would:

"…I'm sorry, I'm very sorry…that was a beautiful apology. You gotta love a guy who can apologize so nice. I rehearsed for over an hour. That's the most you should expect from life, Sandy, a really good apology for all the things you won't get."[1]

There is within each of us, I suspect, a feeling that somebody owes us an apology for all the things we don't get. For all the times things didn't work out as we had planned. For all the times we were denied what we sought to make us happy.

In the movie, *The Big Chill*, Alex, a member of a small group of friends, commits suicide. At the end of his funeral, another friend steps up to the church organ to play Alex's favorite song, ironically, "You Can't Always Get What You Want," made famous by the Rolling Stones. As the movie progresses, the group of friends get together for a reunion, fifteen years later, to take a look at what they each wanted, got, and didn't get over the past years. Have you taken that kind of inventory of your own life?

There is a poem I have found to be meaningful and helpful. Its author unknown:

I asked God for strength, that I might achieve,
I was made weak, that I might learn humbly to obey
I asked for health, that I might do greater things,
I was given infirmity, that I might do better things.
I asked for riches, that I might be happy,
I was given poverty, that I might be wise.
I asked for power, that I might have the praise of men,
I was given weakness, that I might feel the need of God
I asked for all things, that I might enjoy life,
I was given life, that I might enjoy all things
I got nothing that I asked for--but everything I had hoped for,
Almost despite myself, my unspoken prayers were answered.
I am among all men, most richly blessed.

Would it really be good for us to get everything we want or ask God for? Sometimes God may refuse to give us what we ask for in order to give us something greater. Paul prayed three times to have the thorn in

[1] Herb Gardner, *A Thousand Clowns*, (New York: Random House, 1962).

his flesh removed, but each time God said to him, "My grace is sufficient for you, for power is made perfect in weakness" (II Cor 12:9). He asked for the removal of his physical problem, but instead he received the power to triumph over it.

We say, "God never promised you a rose garden." In fact, God told Adam and Eve that life East of Eden was an existence of toil and trouble, thorns and thistles, living by the sweat of our brow. No rose garden. God never promised any of us an existence free from pain and struggle. Even some of the greatest people to ever live. Moses, for one. I wonder if anyone ever said "I'm sorry" to him? It certainly didn't work out as he had planned. After forty years of listening to grumbling and mumbling in the wilderness, Moses finally gets to the Promised Land. Finally! We're here! But—Moses goes up to the top of Mount Nebo, and from there he could see the whole Promised Land. All of it. And God said to him, "This is the land of which I swore to Abraham, to Isaac, and to Jacob, saying, 'I will give it to your descendants'; I have let you see it with your eyes, but you shall not cross over there" (Deut 34:4). And Moses dies, not in the Promised Land, but in the land of Moab, never having reached his ultimate goal in life. Just as Martin Luther King would one day echo those words, "I have seen the Promised Land. I may not get there with you…"

The writer of Hebrews adds others to the list of those for whom life was not living in Disneyland. Persons of great faith "…were stoned to death, they were sawn in two, they were killed by the sword; they went about in skins of sheep and goats, destitute, persecuted, tormented…" (Heb 11:37). Not only did they endure that, but they "...did not receive what was promised…" (Heb 11:39). They never had all their dreams come true. All their wishes fulfilled. All their plans brought to fruition.

One of my favorite passages of scripture is found in the third chapter of Habakkuk. I love the "in spite of" kind of faith and trust. "Even though," "no matter that," "nevertheless." It is the shout of "Hallelujah, anyhow."

Though the fig tree does not blossom,
and no fruit is on the vines;
though the produce of the olive fails,
and the fields yield no food;
though the flock is cut off from the fold,
and there is no herd in the stalls,
yet I will rejoice in the LORD;

I will exult in the God of my salvation. (Hab 3:17-18)

There's another poem that has been of enormous help to me, written by Annie Johnson Flint in 1919:

God hath not promised
Skies always blue,
Flower-strewn pathways
All our lives through;
God hath not promised
Sun without rain,
Joy without sorrow,
Peace without pain.
But God hath promised
Strength for the day,
Rest for the labor,
Light for the way,
Grace for the trials,
Help from above,
Unfailing sympathy,
Undying love.

That, my friends, God guarantees.

Questions for Contemplating and Conversing

1. Do you still receive (and look through) catalogues?
2. Do you receive seed catalogues? If so, what do you do with them?
3. Why do so many of our hopes and dreams and plans turn into disappointments?
4. Do *planning* and *planting* both involve expectations? In what way?
5. Does the world owe you an apology? Does God? Why or why not?
6. What is the main lesson you learned from this chapter?

17. The Smallest Seed and Our Biggest Need

"The central goal of Jesus' life was to plant the seed of this new kingdom so that, like a mustard seed, it would gradually expand…"

–Greg Boyd[1]

There have been times, when adopting a budget that obviously was beyond income projections, someone on a finance committee has said, "We need to have faith that we can meet the budget." It has always surprised me to hear someone talk about "faith" in a discussion that focuses on financial facts and figures. It shouldn't be that unusual to hear about faith in the church, but it is. We often tend to go about our business as if there were no God. The same is unfortunately true in life. Jesus would have us change our way of thinking and of living: "He put before them another parable: 'The kingdom of heaven is like a mustard seed that someone took and sowed in his field; it is the smallest of all the seeds, but

[1] Gregory A. Boyd, *The Myth of a Christian Nation: How the Quest for Political Power Is Destroying the Church*, (Grand Rapids: Zondervan, 2007), 9.

when it has grown it is the greatest of shrubs and becomes a tree, so that the birds of the air come and make nests in its branches" (Mt 13: 31 – 32).

"The apostles said to the Lord, 'Increase our faith!' The Lord replied, "If you had faith the size of a mustard seed, you could say to this mulberry tree, 'Be uprooted and planted in the sea,' and it would obey you" (Lk 17: 5 – 6).

Have you ever seen a begonia seed? It's one of the smallest seeds there is. I gave up planting them because they are so tiny and I am sure I've accidentally thrown away a number of them hiding in the corner of the envelope when it was discarded. As hard as they are to see, they are even harder to sow, and it has never ceased to amaze me how such tiny seeds can produce plants so bountifully blessed with blooms. In one of my books on growing flowers from seed, a horticulturist writes, "There are times when it seems ludicrous to suggest that the dust in the corner of a packet of begonia seed will eventually be transformed into big bushy plants." It has felt that way to me.

Jesus seemed to notice the small things in life. Like the hairs of a person's head, the tiny birds of the air, the flowers of a field, lost coins, a widow's mite, a cup of cold water. When he conducted his object lesson about the mustard seed, I suspect he passed one around to show the crowd, or maybe stood by a full-grown mustard plant. He might have done both, saying, "See this seed? Really itsy-bitsy, teeny-tiny, isn't it? See that shrub with the birds nesting in it? Same plant! Amazing, isn't it? The kingdom of heaven is like that. Your faith should be like that."

One of the smallest seeds, the mustard plant grew to a height of 8 to 10 feet. Birds are attracted to its shade and branches. Though often treated as a parable of growth, I think Jesus was pointing out the sharp contrast between the initial and final form of the mustard. It seemed ludicrous to believe that tiny seed would become an impressive shrub. But somehow the mustard is transformed, defying expectations and initial appearances.

(I understand that the mustard seed is not the world's smallest seed. The smallest plant known is the Wolffia. It floats on the surface of ponds and is also known as duckweed. Five thousand of them can be packed into a thimble. The seed is smaller than a grain of salt.)

When the disciples asked Jesus to increase their faith--or as we might say, improve their attitude--he told them, "If you had faith the size of a mustard seed, you could say to this mulberry tree, 'Be uprooted and planted in the sea,' and it would obey you." The mustard seed has been a symbol of hope, positive expectation, faith and patience. Most of us aren't interested in moving mulberry trees from our yards to the sea, (we mostly just put a chain saw to them), but we have long lists of other things we want to happen and want to accomplish in life. Jesus says an encouraging word to us. Faith like that can give us a different perspective. It can give us the motivation and confidence so necessary to fulfilling our goals.

The first thing we could learn from this parable about the mustard seed is that our outlook at the beginning has a lot to do with the outcome at the end. Having faith can mean believing something will happen just as we want it to. The "conceive--believe--achieve" popular-saying sort of thing. In the KJV, a Proverb puts it, "As a man thinketh in his heart so is he" (Prov 23:7). A poem reminds us:

> Mind is the master-power that molds and makes,
> And man is mind, and evermore he takes
> The tool of thought, and, shaping what he wills,
> brings forth a thousand joys, a thousand ills.
> He thinks in secret and it comes to pass...[2]

There were two talking buckets in a well. The first said, "This is a terrible life; I come up full and go back down empty." The other said, "It's not so bad; I go down empty and come back up full." Attitude is important. Perspective is crucial. Golfer Gary Player used to tell people what he thought of their golf courses, but it got everyone so upset that he began to say they've all got the greatest courses in the world. But the surprising thing was what happened to him. He said, "If I think the course is lousy, I play lousy golf. But if I convince myself it's great, I don't spend my time out there thinking how bad it is."

Unlike magnets, positive attracts positive. Negative thoughts don't attract anything but more negative forces. There does seem to be a cumulative effect to events and experiences, and so we often say something like "I'm on a roll," or “I'm in a slump." Someone has said, "When you believe something is impossible, your mind goes to work for you to prove why, But, when you believe, really believe, something can be done, your mind goes to work for you and helps you to find the ways to do it." In that sense, the mind serves as a cheerleader, calling out, "You can do it." So often we are like the fellow whose car barely made the grade of a steep hill. When it finally reached the summit, the driver turned to his wife and said, "I don't think we'd ever have made it if I hadn't kept one

[2] "As a Man Thinketh" in a literary essay by James Allen, published in 1903

foot on the brakes to keep us from rolling backward!" We hold ourselves back because our "foot is on the brake," and we are more afraid of failing or falling back than in moving full speed ahead.

William James said, "Our belief at the beginning of a doubtful undertaking is the one thing that assures the successful outcome of our venture." Ralph Waldo Emerson said, "Belief is absolutely necessary; no accomplishment, no assistance, no training can compensate for lack of belief." What we do is formulate a mental picture of ourselves succeeding whenever we set a goal or begin a task. The little poem, "Thinking," reminds us that,

> If you think you are beaten, you are;
> If you think you dare not, you don't.
> If you want to win but don't think you can,
> It's almost a cinch you won't.[3]

A good many of us feel "whipped" before we ever attempt anything because our self-talk has beaten us down.

Picturing the desired result as already being accomplished is like priming an old hand pump. To prime a pump, one has to pour water in the top, wait a few minutes, raise and lower the handle in short strokes until the suction pipe fills with water. Being positive about the outcome of an endeavor is like priming the pump.

There's no question that it is better to live with positive attitudes and great expectations than with negativism and indifference. We will never succeed when we imagine ourselves as failures. There's a little piece that made the rounds of businesses, sent by e-mail titled "Attitude Is Everything." It's about a fellow named Jerry who was always in a good mood and always had something positive to say. He was asked how he was always so positive. He responded,

> Each morning I wake up and say to myself, Jerry, you have two choices today. You can choose to be in a good mood or you can choose to be in a bad mood. I choose to be in a good mood. Each time something bad happens, I can choose to be a victim or I can choose to learn from it. I choose to learn from it. Every time someone comes to me complaining, I can choose to accept their complaining or I can point out the positive side of life. I choose

[3] Walter D. Wintle, "Thinking," 1905, Unity Tract Society.

the positive side of life. Life is all about choices. It's your choice how you live life. Attitude, after all, is everything.

Attitude is everything. That is like the story of the young boy who had to play baseball by himself. He would take his bat and ball to the back yard and start his own game. He would throw the ball into the air and swing with all his might. He would often say to himself, “I’m the greatest baseball hitter of all time.” One time, he threw the ball up, tried to hit it, and missed. He yelled out, “Strike one!” He retrieved the ball and threw it into the air and swung again. He missed, so “Strike two!” echoed through the yard. The third time he tried to hit it but missed. “Strike three, you’re out!” Undaunted, he held his head up high and yelled for all the world to hear, “I’m the greatest pitcher of all time!”

Having said all that, we should also acknowledge that positive attitudes can only take us so far. Two hunters were looking for ducks when a flock of geese flew overhead. One man, who was a notoriously bad shot, emptied his shotgun in their direction. They continued flying untouched. The man, though, who was a follower of Robert Schuller's possibility thinking, turned to his friend and said, "Would you look at that! Dead birds flying!"

There are some limits to the power of positive thinking. There are some situations which cannot change just by changing one's attitude. We cannot deny reality. That is where what Jesus said about the mustard seed comes in. Jesus spoke, and Matthew wrote, to those who had hoped for so much and who saw so little happen. The growth from seed to plant was not just an example of growth and continuity, but of contrast. He might have asked, "Would you expect this to amount to that?" Something that held no promise commensurate with such an outcome spoke of the need for faith. The tiniest of seeds contained a message to meet our greatest need.

That need is for more faith. The writer of Hebrews said, "Now faith is the assurance of things hoped for, the conviction of things not seen" (Heb 11:1). Someone has said hope is "the dream of an improbably prosperous outcome." Augustine said, "Faith is to believe what we do not see." A hiker came across a downhearted fisherman casting his hook, line and sinker into the waters of a stream. The hiker asked, "Do you fish here much?" "Yes, all the time," the fisherman answered. "What do you fish for?" "Bass, mostly." "What size?" "Oh, anything up to five pounds." "What do they look like?" "I have no idea," the honest fisherman said.

Faith works in those situations when we feel like saying, "I have no idea how this is going to work out right." Simply put, faith is the acknowledgement that "tall oaks from little acorns grow." It reminds us that one cannot predict the outcome of a less-than-promising beginning. It focuses on the sharp contrast between the initial and final state. After all, Jesus might say, who would have predicted that an entire people would have sprung from such humble beginnings as a single seed of faith planted in the heart of Abraham? A colleague and friend in Pennsylvania, Eric Ritz, reminds us that "today's Christian community of 2.4 billion people began with 12 obscure men… The American civil rights movement began when Rosa Parks refused to move to the back of the bus…Habitat for Humanity began with Millard Fuller recommitting his life to Jesus Christ."

As further illustrations of the significance of small beginnings, Eric wrote that the Mayflower only carried 101 people! Think of what came of that!

Greg Boyd called it “the mustard seed revolution,” a movement that would grow and eventually take over the world.

To that list, I would add the story of how Jean Henri Dunant became involved in giving aid on the battlefields of Italy over 150 years ago, and that became the impetus for the world's first rescue society, called the Red Cross. A snowflake stopped Napoleon in his invasion of Russia. A snowflake defeated him at Waterloo. A mosquito halted the construction of the Panama Canal. A tiny atom changed the way we fought wars. In 1910, eighteen-year-old Joyce Hall left Nebraska with two shoeboxes full of picture postcards. From that the Hallmark Card Company now produces ten million cards every day.

Remember the old song, “Little Things Mean a Lot”? Who would have imagined what would come from an experiment in a storm back in 1752, when Ben Franklin stretched a silk handkerchief across two sticks and attached a metal wire at one end and a metal key at the other--and drew a small electric spark? Or that a beverage mixer invented in 1922, which came to be known as a Waring Blender, would eventually help Jonas Salk combat polio when he used it to grind up materials needed to prepare cultures for a polio vaccine? Or that the modern-day copy machine would have evolved from an invention developed in an apartment kitchen during the Depression--rejected by IBM, GE, and RCA; described by critics, as "interesting, but has no future"--but which helped turn a little company in Rochester, New York, into the Xerox Corporation? Those examples of small beginnings which grew into something of lasting significance ought to encourage us when we want instant results or are tempted to give up on some dream too soon.

A little girl was asked by her teacher, "Debbie, how many great persons were born in our city?" The girl answered, "There were no great persons born in our city. They were born babies who became great persons."

In his book, *The Mustard Seed Conspiracy*, Tom Sine writes:

> God's strategy--changing the world through the conspiracy of the insignificant...He chose a ragged bunch of Semite slaves to become the insurgents of his new order…He chose an undersized shepherd boy with a slingshot to lead his chosen people. And who would have ever dreamed that God would choose to work through a baby in a cow stall to turn this world right side up! It is still God's policy to work through the embarrassingly insignificant to change his world and create his future.[4]

Faith does not operate in the realm of the possible. It begins where our power and potential end--and God's promises begin. So often you and I work to "have it all nailed down," "our ducks all in a row," "the necessary votes in our pocket," before we attempt anything. That surely leaves little room for God to work.

That's why faith involves, and depends upon, trust. What faith does is invite God into the equation. A minister tells of a conversation he had with his brother, who told him, "If the Lord would give me wings, I would fly." He replied, "If the Lord bid me fly, I should trust him for the wings." To trust God does not always mean we are able to see how things will work out, or to see the outcome clearly, but to believe things will work out right in the end. Former Michigan State football coach Duffy Daugherty told of a field goal his kicker Dave Kaiser made against UCLA which gave the Spartans a 17-14 win. Daugherty noticed Kaiser didn't watch the ball after he kicked it. "You're right coach, I didn't watch the ball. I was watching the referee to see how he would call it. You see, I forgot my contact lenses at the hotel. I couldn't even see the goal posts." At first Daugherty was angry, but then he realized that Kaiser had confidence that he would make the goal posts, even when he couldn't see them.

Do you remember when tiny mustard seeds encased in a little container were a popular piece of jewelry? Many of us treat our faith in the same

[4] Tom Sine, *The Mustard Seed Conspiracy: You Can Make a Difference in Tomorrow's World* (Waco: Word, 1981).

way. We carry it around with us, but it is nothing more than an accessory. Once a weekend gardener showed an out-of-town visitor the packets of seed he had ordered. They promised huge, tasty vegetables of every kind. He boasted, "This will be my best garden ever." Later that summer the same friend dropped by for another visit and asked, "How is your garden doing?" "I'm sorry to say it hasn't done very well," the gardener replied. "What was the problem? Bad soil? Pests? Dry weather?" The man shook his head. "Then maybe your seed was the problem." "Yeah, I guess the seed was the problem. I never got around to planting any of it."

Take what little bit of faith you may have, and plant it. Plant it wherever you are in doubt about the success of your dreams and desires, how they will turn out. Many times, we do not utilize the faith we have already been given. We only attempt what we know to be humanly possible, or within our powers. When is the last time you tried something that was impossible unless God got involved? Jesus once asked some blind men if they believed he could heal them. They both said yes, so Jesus told them, "According to your faith be it done to you." Not according to facts, or fate, but their faith.

Sometimes prayer is the greatest affirmation of faith we can make. And its eventual influence and impact can have far-reaching effects. Just one illustration of that. There was a mother who prayed daily for her wayward son. As she worked at her jobs, often during poverty and illness, she continued to believe and trust in her son's redemption. She remembered the day her son, John, still in his teens, ran away from home to become a sailor--and a very rowdy, wicked man. God heard her prayer and worked a miracle in John Newton's heart. You will recall he was the sailor-preacher who wrote the beloved, "Amazing Grace." Among the thousands of people Newton led to Christ was Thomas Scott, whose life had been a miserable failure. Thomas Scott had a profound influence on William Cowper, who used his talent as a hymn writer to bring thousands of unbelievers to Christ. One of his hymns, "There Is a Fountain," impacted William Wilberforce, who was a great British statesman generally credited with the abolition of slavery in England.

Amazing, isn't it? All that resulted from one mother's prayers for her son. Faith the size of a mustard seed can be a “mountain mover.” I understand there is a powerful plant hormone called brassinolide. It can be used for cell elongation, root growth, seed germination, immunity, reproduction, mediating plant response to stress and disease, and increases in yield. I was surprised to read that using less than one-billionth of an ounce can double the size of plants.

Some scholars believe when Jesus referred to a mustard seed, he was pointing to black mustard. The Talmud, the ancient Jewish commentary on the Old Testament, prohibited planting mustard in a garden because it would quickly take over.

So, Jesus likened the rule of God to a *weed.* We call plants like that "invasive." Perhaps Jesus meant we should let God's will and spirit "invade" our lives: intrude, occupy, subjugate, take over, and conquer!

Questions for Contemplating and Conversing

1. How was the birth of a baby in Bethlehem a "small beginning" that brought about a world-wide movement?
2. What other "small beginnings" have grown into significant developments?
3. Do you sometimes feel that your faith isn't "big enough" and you pray "Increase my faith"?
4. Why do we need faith?
5. Steve Allen wrote a song, "This Could Be the Start of Something Big." Is that your attitude when starting a project or beginning a task?
6. What is the main lesson you learned from this chapter?

18. Is Our Failure in Achieving or Perceiving Success?

"Let us try to see things from their better side:
You complain about seeing thorny rose bushes;
Me, I rejoice and give thanks to the gods
That thorns have roses."

-Attributed to Alphonse Karr

Failures. Maybe I should have kept a list of all my gardening failures. (I can pretty much tell you all the failures I've had in life, even the "F" I received in a high school journalism class for a paper I wrote.) There have been some summers when I would have admitted *I'm a failure at gardening.*

How many of you consider yourselves successful? My next question might be How do you define success? Or maybe successful in what? In your profession? In raising children? As a spouse? In living as a Christian? In fulfilling your membership vows? In doing what God wants you to do?

That same day Jesus went out of the house and sat beside the sea. Such great crowds gathered around him that he got into a boat and sat there, while the whole crowd stood on the beach. And he told them many things in parables, saying: "Listen! A sower went out to sow. And as he sowed, some seeds fell on the path, and the birds came and ate them up. Other seeds fell on rocky ground, where they did not have much soil, and they sprang up quickly, since they had no depth of soil. But when the sun rose, they were scorched; and since they had no root, they withered away. Other seeds fell among thorns, and the thorns grew up and choked them. Other seeds fell on good soil and brought forth grain, some a hundredfold, some sixty, some thirty. Let anyone with ears listen!" (Mt 13:1-9).

"Hear then the parable of the sower. When anyone hears the word of the kingdom and does not understand it, the evil one comes and snatches away what is sown in the heart; this is what was sown on the path. As for what was sown on rocky ground, this is the one who hears the word and immediately receives it with joy; yet such a person has no root, but endures only for a while, and when trouble or persecution arises on account of the word, that person immediately falls away. As for what was sown among thorns, this is the one who hears the word, but the cares of the world and the lure of wealth choke the word, and it yields nothing. But as for what was sown on good soil, this is the one who hears the word and understands it, who indeed bears fruit and yields, in one case a hundredfold, in another sixty, and in another thirty" (Mt 13: 18 – 23).

When I retired from Little League baseball to attend Vacation Bible School, I had a life-time batting average of .000. In fact, I had struck out every time at bat. If you add a couple years playing church league softball, I think my average is something close to .010. I remember getting a hit in one game but was eventually called out at first base for leaving the base too soon.

For a while, I took great comfort in the inauspicious beginning of the career of home run hitter, Hank Aaron. On opening day of the 1954 baseball season, Aaron was a rookie for the Milwaukee Braves; he started in left field and went 0 for 5. From there on, however, his baseball career and mine went in opposite directions.

Babe Ruth may have been the Home Run King, but he also set a major league record for strikeouts, 1330 of them. He also set a record for five consecutive strikeouts in a World Series game. Stan Musial, one of my childhood heroes, failed two out of every three times he stepped up to the plate--his lifetime batting average was less than .340--but he is remembered as being one of the game's greatest hitters. Most serious ballplayers would be happy to bat .250, getting a hit a fourth of the time at the plate. That's probably the only sport in which such a low percentage of success is desirable or even acceptable. A shooting percentage that low in basketball, in either field goals or free throws, would be awful. It would translate to a score of about 75 in bowling. The career of a place-kicker would be short indeed if he only made a fourth of his extra point or field goal attempts.

When it comes to most every other pursuit in life, we fully expect to bat a thousand. Every sermon has to be a home run. Every call on a client has to result in a signed contract. Every lesson taught has to be learned by every student. What kind of doctor would be satisfied with curing only a third of his or her patients' illnesses? What kind of dentist would be satisfied if only half your false teeth fit?

Those of us whose hobby is gardening know all about success and failure. From a disappointing yield of tomatoes to rose bushes that have no blooms, we know what it is to bat less than a thousand. But perhaps the greatest challenge for some of us comes with the germination rates of the seeds we plant. We know that some seeds never produce seedlings, because the seed itself may be infertile, or we may give it the wrong conditions. Most seeds are pretty particular about what we call optimum "time and clime." For instance, some must be grown at fairly high temperatures, others prefer it cool. Some need light to germinate, others prefer it dark. Some seeds need to be soaked, others germinate more quickly if they are rubbed with sandpaper or slit to weaken the seedcoat. Some like to be scattered on top of the soil, others buried. And all of them do best if they are planted in a sterilized planting medium, kept from drying out and from becoming overcrowded.

As much as I try to provide the proper conditions, my success rate with seed sowing is certainly never 100%. But it is certainly much better than the fellow's in the story Jesus told. Think about it: he batted .250; his average was 25%.

Before we judge the sower in the parable as being terribly inefficient in sowing seeds on soil that was a beaten-down pathway, or rocky, or in the middle of a weed patch, it might be good to recall farming was quite hit-or-miss back then. The land was the major obstacle; it is hilly, sloping, and rocky. An old legend says that an angel carrying bags of stones to assist God in creation accidentally dropped one of the bags over Palestine, so half the world's rocks fell on that little stretch of land. The climate was another challenge, since months of heat can pass without a single drop of rain. Additionally, farmers planted by the broadcast method. They had no planting machines to sow neatly in a row, or a Burpee's seed tape to make it more foolproof. Some sowers hung a bag of seed on a mule, tore a small hole in the bag, and then led the animal back and forth through the field, spilling seed with every step. Others sowed by hand, like we sow grass seed. Or how we use a broadcast spreader to fertilize the lawn--which I have done, usually also fertilizing my share of sidewalks and driveways. Some farmers in Jesus' day sowed a grain field by broadcasting the seeds, then plowing them into the soil. When the plow scratched the thin surface of soil above it, even then the seeds would encounter a variety of fates. Birds would eat those that fell on the path not plowed. A shelf of rock would be revealed. Thistle seeds would also be turned under and spring up to choke the grain. But where the soil was good, the yield might be enormous.

This parable probably had a dual function, to exhort listeners and to encourage speakers. Truth is, we are both. We may slip in and out of those roles many times a day. When we are listeners, we can hear that story and ask which of the four kinds of soil we are. The traditional application of this parable is that the sower is God, the seeds are God's Word, and the soil is our heart, soul, and mind. The challenge is for us to be "good soil," receptive and open to hearing and doing the Word of God.

This parable can speak to the other times when we don't seem to be getting as much out of some experience as we should. The problem may not be with the message or with the messenger, but with us. Our minds may be like well-worn pathways. You can't plant grass seed underneath a swing set! We cannot concentrate on several things at once. We often have too many things on our minds and too much competes for our attention. Our minds grow numb from being bombarded with information. Other times they are closed, either by mental laziness or arrogance. We shut out unfamiliar or uncomfortable ideas. We resist being made to think. Sometimes our receptivity is too shallow or our commitment too tentative. We may have only good intentions which, without deep roots, can wither under all of life's stresses. Then Jesus said there are times when our minds are like a weed patch. Someone has said that a batch of seedlings had a short life because of "the company they kept." Weeds overtook the good plants, and since they were stronger, these invaders choked the life out of them. There were over 200 species of undesirable weeds in the average farm plot in Jesus' day. Jesus compared those thorns to the cares of the world, delight in riches, and the desire for things. A schoolboy read a list of the chief causes of death and discovered a new fatal disease unknown to him. Asked what it was, he spelled out the word "miscellaneous." You see, it's often the miscellaneous things in life that take over and leave no room for the more important things in life. All the knocks on the door, the phone calls, the demands for attention, the distractions and interruptions that steal from us our best intentions to concentrate on the task at hand. In so many ways, we see ourselves in those types of soil.

But I think most of us would identify with the sower. Anyone who ever speaks to someone else or seeks to communicate effectively knows how the sower felt. Any number of us can see ourselves in him: preachers, teachers, parents, salespersons. Parents realize that not all the seeds they "plant" in their children come to maturity. Some of it never even comes up. Most of the words spoken by the preacher do nothing but bounce off the walls of the sanctuary, or off those whose minds are closed or cluttered. We may feel that three-fourths of our efforts are wasted most of the time. In those times of discouragement, when our work seems futile or fruitless, and when we feel we've failed, Jesus offers us encouragement: "In spite of the risks and rocky times, the failures and frustrations, what you do is worthwhile. Your work is worth the effort. There is always the possibility of an abundant yield despite apparent or immediate results. After all, if you don't sow, you won't reap. What you don't sow, can never grow." Jesus would have us remember that the fruitfulness of the 25% can more than make up for the lack of success with the rest. He was emphasizing those who receive, not those who resist or reject: The children whom we DO reach, the sales we DO make, the good that we DO accomplish. The difference we DO make.

There are any number of lessons to be learned from this little story. For one thing, no one is going to achieve success in everything attempted. You can't win 'em all. You can't come out on top every time out. But often our sense of failure is not in failing to *achieve* success, it is in failing to *perceive* what success really is. It is essential we be realistic in evaluating our efforts. One day a man came into a church and the preacher noticed he had on only one shoe; the other foot was bare. The minister said, "I see you have lost a shoe." The man replied, "No, I found a shoe." It's all in how you look at it: we can see the bare foot, or the foot with the shoe. This is a parable of success, really, not failure.

Once, when Jesus returned to his hometown of Nazareth to teach, to preach, to heal and to recruit disciples, Mark notes, "And he could do no mighty work there, except that he laid his hands upon a few sick people and cured them. And he was amazed at their unbelief" (Mk 6:5-6). He left without a large following enlisted for God's Kingdom. In fact, those who had known him as a little boy playing in his father's carpentry shop, "took offense at him." He failed with his own people. No one responded as he had hoped. He had failed to do any "mighty work there except...except...that he laid his hands upon a few sick people and healed them." I suspect if you had asked one of those folks he healed how they felt about his ministry in Nazareth, they would have called him a resounding success.

There is, also, a word of encouragement in that not every failure is our fault. Jesus failed that one time because of other people. The sower failed three times out of four because of conditions beyond his control. Not every environment is conducive to success. And yet, even though Jesus achieved no "mighty work," he was able to do something of significance. Don't we all agree Mother Teresa is one of the most successful women in the world?

A time management expert has said that it is obvious you can't get everything done that needs to be done, so it's better to spend more time on some activities in areas which are going to have the greatest value and biggest pay-off. Too many of us live life by the broadcast or shot gun method, failing to focus our efforts in the place of the greatest promise.

That would make it tempting for the preacher to take his or her top twenty percent and spend all the time with them. Or to start a whole new church with them. I suspect most doctors would like to treat only the portion of his or her patients who have a chance of making a full recovery. But life isn't like that. Few of us can be so selective and choosy. And so, Jesus' parable offers us another helpful reminder. We never know the effect and influence and payoff of so many of our efforts or so much of the time spent with others. A few years back a member of the church I served in Rushville wrote about a children's sermon during which I gave each child a little mum plant from my garden. She told how she planted it near her house and "each fall we have a large bouquet of mums by our home from those little plants. I am sure this is just one brief story about the results of the many seeds of Christianity." The truth is, we never know how and when the seeds we have scattered in life will take root and bear fruit. One teacher said, "Good teachers are in love with the task of sowing the seed and are content to leave the harvesting to someone else. They spend years sowing seed but hardly ever get to be there for the harvest."

I was in a group of young parents a few years back, and most of them told how so many of their plans for family gatherings and quality time together end up being chaotic, disappointing and an obvious waste of time. They said their expectations may have been too high and their efforts to do things right just didn't have the results they wanted. But they went on to say they were still amazed how their children remembered some of the little things that happened. The least likely event so often becomes precisely the thing that can have the greatest impact, whereas the seemingly most likely event is not the one that does that at all. I guess that's why we have to be extravagant, maybe even wasteful, with our time and efforts. We never know what might take root. Neither does God, so Nature produces more seed than can possibly germinate and come to maturity.

A good friend in a church I had served wrote me about being in the sanctuary with a young mother and her small son. The mother was overheard to tell him, "Here's a special song mommy sang right in this room when I was your age." She sang it word for word, my friend said, like it had been yesterday. It was "The Little Gray Sparrow." She had sung it to me on my last Sunday there, in 1977. We may never know the importance of modest experiences like that.

Finally, this parable of Jesus is relevant to our role as those who are to spread the Word of God. Few of us think of ourselves as sowers of that seed. We may have been discouraged by any efforts we made to witness to our faith, or to bring others to Christ. I'll admit evangelism is much like the farmer sowing three-fourths of his seed on unproductive soil. In one church, the associate pastor in charge of outreach told me that the Evangelism Committee had calculated over one year, they'd personally contacted over one hundred visitors, but only 18 of them joined the church. Was that worth the effort? Granted, so much of what we do does not seem very efficient or effective if measured by the kind productivity we have come to expect from years of technological progress. But human relationships defy that kind of measurement of success. So does a relationship with God.

I think it's very hard to measure success in the ministry and the church. How do we define it? The number of lives changed? The number who worship, who join? The amount of money given? The size of the structure? The number of lives touched? A Bishop once told me that successful ministry is simply "effective ministry."

We are to sow good seed in the world. We are to plant seeds of faith. That doesn't mean buttonholing folks and asking, "Are you saved?" It may just mean you care enough to listen to them.

You know the statistics. I've seen it said that from 40% to 80% of Americans are unchurched. Over half of them say they'd come to church if invited. Another poll said that 61% of all Americans who are not church members claim to be Christians; they simply have not found their way into a caring fellowship where they feel they can belong. Richard Wilke has said that on any given Sunday, about 175 million Americans are not in worship. In one denomination, a church historian said that the average member invites someone else to church once every 28 years! That is in spite of the fact that each of us knows at least eight unchurched persons with whom we have regular contact: neighbors, friends, people at work, relatives. A recent survey reported that Jesus' command to make disciples ranks far down the list of important church functions. Only 32% of us consider evangelism a "very important" activity—far below youth programs, worship and helping the needy. We also know that of ten people who come to a church and stay, nine were invited or brought by a friend. Even knowing that, for too long churches have had a "wait and see" style of evangelism, passively waiting for outsiders to take the first step—while Jesus called us to a "go-and-seek" style of evangelism.

I think it's encouraging that lay people are taking this whole idea of outreach and hospitality and welcoming and inviting more seriously. One church calls it "bringing and including," which is a phrase they use rather than evangelism. For too long we have been like Flip Wilson, who was asked about his denominational affiliation, and he said, "I am a Jehovah's spectator! I would be a witness but that would require too much commitment."

To bring others to Jesus Christ. To invite someone to "come and see for yourself." That is the essence of evangelism and Christian witnessing. Nothing else is necessary. No theological dissertations. No arguing. No coercion. Just an invitation and a simple gesture of wanting to share with another what you have found to be meaningful. After all, don't we tell a friend about a good movie we've seen, or a good restaurant where we've eaten, or a new store that has what we are looking for? Why not tell them about the most important thing in the world? John Ed Mathison has said, "If people are excited about something, they will invite others to share it."

Isn't it sad that not everyone knows what we know, whom we know? Isn't it sad that not everyone has heard the good news? How long can we continue to speak of the gospel as Good News, and talk about how sharing that Good News is one of the fundamental tasks of a congregation, and keep so silent? Surely, if we truly believed we have heard some good news, we would not just timidly whisper about it to our neighbors, we would go running out of here to invite them to "come and see." We'd at least start to sow the seeds, wouldn't we?

Questions for Contemplating and Conversing

1. What is your "batting average" in life when it comes to successes and failures?
2. Have you ever thought of yourself as a failure? Why and when?
3. In what ways have you been successful?
4. Are there times in your life that you have been surprised by the eventual significance of something you thought insignificant?
5. What criteria do you use when labeling someone a success or a failure? Do you use the same criteria for labeling your undertakings?
6. Have you ever been involved in bringing someone to Christ?
7. What is the main lesson you learned from this chapter?

19. Looking for Volunteers

"Vision…must be combined with venture. It is not enough to stare up the steps, we must step up the stairs."

-Vaclav Havel

In his book, *Crockett's Flower Garden,* Jim Crockett, the long-time host of the PBS program, *The Victory Garden,* wrote about Sweet Williams. (It obviously wasn't about me.) That particular flower is a biennial, meaning that it lasts two years. Crockett said that if Sweet Williams are allowed to go to seed, the plants will self-sow. The seedlings will survive winter if mulched, adding that home gardeners may feel inclined to "save a few volunteers and let them mature."[1] You may know that many other plants provide us with volunteers. If you grow tomatoes, and don't pick all the ripe ones in the fall, they very often fall to the ground, rot, and the seeds will germinate the next spring and you will see lots of little tomato seedlings springing up in your garden plot. Volunteers.

[1] James Crockett, *Crockett's Flower Garden* (Boston: Little, Brown and Company, 1981), 127.

The dictionary says that any action that is "voluntary" means that whatever is done is done of our own free will. Plants who are volunteers grow spontaneously without direct human control or supervision, often as seeds lost from a previous crop. Persons who are volunteers enter into service of their own free will. You probably know all about the late President H. W. Bush's efforts to pass the Citizen Service Act, which was to reform and expand community-volunteering programs. Volunteer service was a big part of his agenda for our nation. One of the bill's sponsors said it is about giving something back to the country, in contrast to the examples of corporate greed we see from executives who only ask what they can take for themselves.

I confess that I am frugal. I am always on the lookout for volunteers in my garden. They seem to be nature's bonus for all the work we do in sowing, cultivating and nurturing. They are often pleasant surprises. I have a friend who called me one spring day to ask about some little plants that had popped up in her hanging basket left outside over the winter. I had the pleasure of informing her that she had some left-over petunias from the year before. I explained about volunteers. She let them grow and some weeks later told me how beautiful the plants had become.

Pastors are always on the lookout for volunteers in the church. They often go through a process of *drafting* volunteers. That may seem a contradiction in terms, but that's how it is in the church these days. Too few just "step up to the plate."

"Then he said to his disciples, 'The harvest is plentiful, but the laborers are few; therefore, ask the Lord of the harvest to send out laborers into his harvest'" (Mt 9:35-38).

I don't recall very many times when a member of the church called me or stopped by to volunteer for a job in the church. That is always a pleasant surprise. It happens that way occasionally, but more often than not, we have to initiate the contact and frequently use our powers of persuasion. I learned early on not to say "It's an easy job. Anyone can do it. That's why we are asking you." That's not only an insult, but it does little to motivate anyone. I have found more people respond to a challenging opportunity. Most of us want to be a part of something significant. That's why I like a proposal Leonard Sweet has made. He said we should quit using the term "volunteer" and start using "minister" instead. Like Minister of Food, Minister of Sound, Minister of Singing, Minister of Lawn Care.

The United Methodist Church has always thought like that. There's a whole section in our *Discipline* about the "Ministry of All Christians." It makes it clear that "All Christians are called to a ministry of servanthood in the world. All Christians are called to minister wherever Christ would have them serve…"

The truth is, too few persons understand they have been "called to the ministry." They leave most everything up to the preacher. There's an old story that may illustrate why that concept doesn't work anymore. One preacher said he got a phone call from a lady who asked if he was a blood donor. He answered that he did give blood occasionally, so she said, "Well, Aunt Callie's doctor phoned from the hospital this morning, and she needs some blood. You know how hard my husband has to work, so I wondered if you'd be willing to give blood." The preacher said he would, and he did, but he wondered what would happen if someone had called the next day with the same request. It wouldn't be long before he needed a "refill" himself.

It's not humanly possible for one or two persons to fulfill the ministry of a congregation. There is so much to do in any congregation. I used to have a sign I posted on my office door. I think I originally got it for use in emergencies in my car. It said, in bold letters, "SEND HELP."

Every pastor I know of could use some help.

I would always consider myself a "player/coach." I'm tried to do my part, even as I encouraged others to do theirs. As much as I might wish I could be the manager, pitch the ball, run behind the plate to catch it, and when the ball is hit, to run into the outfield to make the out—it just can't be done.

That was something of the situation facing Moses. Moses had led the people of Israel through the wilderness toward Mt. Sinai, following the Exodus from Egypt. He had been chosen to be their leader. Apparently, he had been reunited with his family, including his father-in-law, and it soon became obvious that Moses was exhausting himself trying to deal with all the administrative problems associated with leading thousands of persons toward the Promised Land. Like herding cats most days, I'd guess. He had fallen into the trap of all leaders, attempting to be all things to all people, omni-competent and responsible for all the problems that arose among the people. He couldn't keep up and the people were deprived of the attention they deserved in resolving their problems. He was spending less and less time doing what he really needed to be doing: staying in close touch with God. Even more, the competent individuals within that group were deprived of the opportunity to use their God-given talents. His father-in-law, Jethro, watched what was happening to Moses, and when he couldn't stand to see it anymore, he took him aside and had a father-son talk with him.

> "What you are doing is not good. You will surely wear yourself out, both you and these people with you. For the task is too heavy for you; you cannot do it alone. Now listen to me. I will give you counsel, and God be with you! You should represent the people before God, and you should bring their cases before God; teach them the statutes and instructions and make known to them the way they are to go and the things they are to do. You should also look for able men among all the people, men who fear God, are trustworthy, and hate dishonest gain; set such men over them as officers over thousands, hundreds, fifties and tens. Let them sit as judges for the people at all times; let them bring every important case to you but decide every minor case themselves. So, it will be easier for you, and they will bear the burden with you. If you do this, and God so commands you, then you will be able to endure, and all these people will go to their home in peace" (Ex 18:17-23).

So, Moses paid attention and chose able persons to assist him, still willing to deal with the major decisions, but they handled a lot of the minor details themselves.

An even more significant aspect of the challenge is spiritual, not just practical. It is absolutely basic to our Christian Faith to affirm that every Christian has been called and given gifts for ministry.

Have you ever thought of yourself as "gifted and called by God"? Your giftedness is one of the most significant messages of the New Testament. In his first letter to the Corinthians, Paul wrote: "Now concerning spiritual gifts, brothers and sisters, I do not want you to be uninformed" (I Cor 12:1). Unfortunately, most people in the church today *are* uninformed about spiritual gifts. A recent Gallup Poll reported that only ten per cent of American church members are active in any kind of personal ministry. There are at least five places in the New Testament in which they are listed: gifts of serving, of teaching, of giving, of leading, or working miracles, of faith, of helping, of healing, of administrating, or evangelism, and so on. They are also referred to as our "creation gifts."

God has given us all gifts for ministry. There's not a single person who has not been given a gift for ministry. In his letter to the Ephesians, Paul tells us: "The gifts (God) gave were…to equip the saints for the work of ministry, for building up the body of Christ" (Eph 4:11-12). Every believer is a minister. Every ministry is important. We need each other.

That's why many congregations are involved in working with members to help them discover their spiritual gifts, focusing on abilities, personality, experience and interests and matching them with needs.

I've always liked the idea that my job in the church is to turn passengers into members of the crew. Customers into owners of the store. Members into ministers. I once heard what a hospital janitor said after becoming friends with one of the physicians there. He said, "Me and Dr. Jones, we are in the business of helping sick people get better." He had obviously caught the vision of what it meant to be a member of a team.

There are congregations which are a literal beehive of activity. Lots of things are going on. But let me tell you about a *real* beehive. Honeybees are highly organized. A beehive may house as many as 80,000 bees, each of which performs a specialized duty. Some are forager bees, which fly great distances to collect food. The guard bees protect the hive entrance from intruders. The scout bees keep the hive alert to opportunities and dangers in the outside world. A few bees even serve as undertakers, responsible for removing dead bodies from the hive. Others are water collectors. They bring in moisture to regulate the hive's humidity. Some are plasterers. Still others are scent fanners who station themselves at the hive entrance and blow the scent outward so that disoriented bees can locate their home base.

Every Christian has received gifts and has a role to play in the *beehive* of the Church.

When that great cathedral at Chartres, in France, was being constructed, the cost of transporting the building stones from the quarries to the church site was as expensive as the stone itself. So, peasants and nobility alike harnessed themselves by the dozens to enormous carts and pulled tons of stone over miles of poor roads for days on end. Everyone joined in by pulling the carts. That beautiful cathedral is a monument to a cooperative effort for everyone to pull together.

God calls person-to-person. We can hang up on God. God might always get a busy signal. But God is persistent in calling us person-to-person. God doesn't get in touch with us with a letter addressed to occupant or current resident. The envelope has our name on it. In fact, in many instances in the Bible, God literally did call out a person's name.

We hear God call out, "Moses! Moses!" "Samuel! Samuel!" "Saul, Saul."

I read somewhere that God's call involves our asking "What does God want me to do?" and "Who does God want me to be?" You may remember the first words spoken over the telephone in 1876 by the inventor, Alexander Graham bell, to Thomas Watson. Bell had spilled acid on his clothing while pouring it into a telephone experimental unit. He called out, "Mr. Watson, come here. I need you." That may be God's message to you: "I need you."

Will you get the message? Back when the telegraph was the fastest method of long-distance communication, a young man applied for a job as Morse code operator. He went to the office listed in the newspaper ad, and entered a large, busy office filled with noise, clutter and the sound of Morse code clicking in the background. He was told to fill out a form and to wait with the seven other applicants until they were called into the inner office. The young man filled in the form and sat down. The office was so noisy no one could talk, so most of the young men sat silently, some reading magazines, others dozing, not paying much attention to what was going on around them. This one young man, however, sat poised and ready to enter the office at the very moment he was called. After a few moments, he stood up, and walked right into the inner office. The other applicants looked up, wondering what was going on. In a few minutes, the employer stepped out. He said to the other seven applicants, "Gentlemen, thank you very much for coming, but the job has just been filled." They were surprised and angry. One of them spoke up, "Wait a minute! I don't understand. He was the last one to come in, and we never even got a chance to be interviewed. Yet he got the job. That's not fair." The employer said to them, "I'm sorry, but all the time you've been sitting here, the telegraph has been ticking out in Morse code: 'If you understand this message, then come right in. The job is yours.' None of you heard it or understood it. This young man did. He was listening. The job is his."

Are you listening? There is a job waiting for you. A fellow was on a flight across the country when the flight attendant asked if he would like dinner. He asked, "What are my choices?" The flight attendant replied, "Yes or no."

Picture God waiting for you to say "yes."

1. Do you have a history of “volunteering”? If so, can you list the jobs/positions you have volunteered for?
2. What is the difference between a volunteer and a recruit?
3. Do you seek new opportunities to be of service of others?
4. Do the organizations to which you belong have an on-going need for people to “step up to the plate?”
5. Who or what really needs you?
6. What is the main lesson you learned from this chapter?

20. Wait'll Next Year?

"A year from now you may wish you had started today."
-Karen Lamb[1]

My sister told me it happened to her about mid-August. It happens for lots of other folks about then, too. For me, it usually coincides with the time department stores put out their back-to-school supplies--or when some of them are putting out their Christmas items--and when school signs change their message from "Have a Happy Summer" to the date students are to report for classes. Some years, it happens when extended dry spells hit, and I get tired of lugging hoses and sprinklers around my yard, when the white flies take up residence in my tomato patch, or I realize the battle with Japanese beetles is not winnable.

What happens is that we give up on our gardens. At some point during late summer, we undergo a shift in our thinking. What was once full of promise and possibility becomes another area of neglect. The garden we carefully kept free from pests and predators is surrendered to them. We may throw up our hands and let the plants go to seed and the garden grow

[1] Karen Lamb, *A Year from Now You May Wish You Had Started Today*, (Independently Published, 2020).

to weeds. We may get tired of such intense attention. We may just grow bored with it all. Regardless, we write off this year and turn our attention to next year. It's when gardeners begin using the phrase those of us who are Cubs' fans made famous: "Wait'll next year!" I love this quote I came across: “A garden is never as good as it will be next year.”

There's a lot of wishful thinking in gardening. I've been told that 95% of gardening is spent leaning on your hoe and dreaming; the other 5% actually working. It's human nature to look ahead and hope. Since things are seldom ever what we want them to be, we need to dream of when they will be. As a poet says, "Life is not, but ever to be, blest."

For weeks avid gardeners deadhead annuals, picking off the spent blooms before they go to seed. It's almost a daily ritual. It lengthens the time the flowers will produce blooms. But late in the summer I do something entirely different. I purposefully let the flowers go to seed so I can collect the seeds for growing plants next year. Some plants self-sow, but others can have their seedpods painstakingly picked, sorted and stored.

Isn't it like that in life? There are times we have to let nature run its course, let it go, and look ahead. Wait till next year. We may try to harvest something of value that will be useful in the future--as we gather seeds for next year's plants--but mostly we just turn away and move on. As someone once said, "There's no use watering last year's crops."

One gardener I know of reminds us that every season gardeners hold countless little funerals. Season after season, as we go about a garden's daily business, we see a thousand little deaths. Vegetables produce their harvest and the plants are killed by frost. A flower shrivels with age. Death in a garden is an expected and essential aspect of existence.

Another garden writer said that human beings have a hard time letting anything go. But when the summer is over, it is time to let the garden go. We take comfort in the knowledge that spring will come and the entire process will begin again. There will be other tomatoes.

Some of the bits of advice we need to hear from time to time are "Let it go. Get over it. Get on with your life. Tomorrow's another day. Move on." There's no use crying over spilt milk, nursing our grievances, hanging on to our grudges, or staring at our scars.

There are other reasons August is a pivotal month, maybe more so than January. It is not just a time for looking ahead to next year, it's a time for looking back and assessing how many times we didn’t get up to answer the door when opportunity knocked. If you didn’t do that during August, September is also a good month for considering how many things we have left undone and how many times we have said, "I guess it'll have to wait till next year." We should take inventory of all the things we put off. Most summers I have a road map covered with destinations I never made it to on a vacation. For too many years my canoe continued its restful inactivity leaning against the house. The golf clubs were hidden behind dusty lawn chairs. My bicycle would hang from the hook where it had been for years. The fishing poles hung forgotten in the garage. There is always a list on my desk of movies I wanted to see over the summer.

I take comfort in knowing I am not the only one with those feelings of in-completion. One popular columnist had an article about his vacation being over. He said, "No one ever wants to hear what anyone else did on vacation so let me tell you some of the things I didn't do." He went on to list things he didn't get done: He didn't read a book, or write a lot of letters, or lose weight, or get a tan, or start raspberry bushes in his garden, or lower the wheels on the lawnmower, or wax his car, or buy a new garbage can lid, come up with a lot of good new ideas, or go to visit Bessie--a dear old family friend. He said, "I wanted to drive up and see her during my vacation, but I never did. I feel bad about it," he concluded.

We are so prone to procrastinate and postpone. We say, "Someday" or "One of these days." Too much of life is going to be lived "next year." It reads like a litany:

Next year I graduate from high school; then I'll...
Next year I'll be twenty-one; then I will...
Next year I'm getting married; then I...
Next year the house gets paid off; then...
Next week I'm going to get a break in my business; then I'll...
Next week I'm going to win the lottery; then I'll...
Next year the children will be grown and out on their own...
Next year I'm going to retire; then...

And so, we make our lists: After school starts. After Labor Day. After Thanksgiving. After Christmas. After the first of the year. Life is a list of "laters," isn't it? Our plans are prefaced with "someday" or "whenever" or "if and when."

Nathaniel Hawthorne wrote notes in his diary for "a story in which the chief character never appears." Some of us live lives like that: we have been waiting for years for someone or something to appear. In some cases, we wait for someone who will be our messiah or savior, making everything right. Ironically, Hawthorne never got around to writing the story!

Robert Frost once offered what he called "A Prayer in Spring."

Oh, give us pleasure in the flowers today;
And give us not to think so far away
As the uncertain harvest; keep us here
All simply in the springing of the year…[2]

Don't we know that the "harvest" is always going to be "uncertain" and so the best thing we can do is to take "pleasure in the flowers today"? The time may never be right for doing what we want to do.

And yet, chances are *we really will* have another opportunity next year. When it comes to the failures and futility of life, there is a great deal of hope in knowing we can wait till next year. Life is always offering us another chance. A gardener has seen everything ruined so many times that he has to trust that where there was a garden once, it can be again. One of Kipling's poems, "Pan in Vermont," says that:

What though his phlox and hollyhocks ere half a month demised?
What though his grapevine clambered not as advertised?
Though every seed was guaranteed and every standard true--
Forget, forgive they did not live! Believe, and buy anew!

That is one of the lessons from Jesus' story about the farmer and the fig tree:

> Then he told this parable: "A man had a fig tree planted in his vineyard; and he came looking for fruit on it and found none. [7]So he said to the gardener, 'See here! For three years I have come looking for fruit on this fig tree, and still I find none. Cut it down! Why should it be wasting the soil?' He replied, 'Sir, let it alone for one more year, until I dig around it and put manure on it. If it bears fruit next year, well and good; but if not, you can cut it down.'" (Lk 13: 6 – 9)

[2] Robert Frost, *The Pocket Book of Robert Frost's Poems*, (New York: Pocket Books, 1956), 259.

I was out in my front yard one day and my neighbor called my attention to a dead-looking plant that she was watering. She said, “It’s hard to believe this thing blooms every year, isn’t it?” She said as dead as it appeared it always came back as a beautiful rhododendron. She resisted the urge to pull it up.

There are times when it's a good thing to "wait'll next year" because we have to learn to be more patient. We give up too soon. I read an article about some seeds that sank in a Spanish galleon 365 years earlier. They sprouted when brought to shore and planted. Can’t we wait on things for a few days or months?

On his radio call-in show, a local gardening expert often says to listeners, "Fertilize your tree and wait another year. It might come back." That's not bad advice for situations and people, either. Jesus always believed in giving someone a second chance. I think that's what this parable is about. The truth is, you and I often cut down others because we give up on them too soon. Their lack of fruitfulness may just mean they are in a dormant state and we need to provide the right conditions for their growth. We should never be too quick to write off anyone because of an apparent lack of promise or potential. A college professor asked his ethics class: "A certain man has syphilis; his wife has tuberculosis; of their four children, one has died, the other three suffer from an illness that is considered terminal. The mother is pregnant. What do you recommend?" After considerable discussion, the recommendation made by the majority of the students was to abort the pregnancy. "It was," as a class member said, "the expedient thing to do." "That is interesting," replied the professor. "You have just kept Beethoven from coming into the world."

Did you know Michael Jordan was cut from his high school freshman basketball team?

In J. B. Phillips’ translation of II Corinthians 4:8, Paul writes, “…we may be knocked down, but we are never knocked out!”[3] There is a difference between being knocked down and knocked out, isn’t there?

I can give you a long list of folks who are really up against it and who are about ready to call it quits. To wave the white flag. To shrug their shoulders and mutter “It’s fruitless; why bother?” To throw in the towel. To walk out. To cave in. To say, “enough is enough.” To ask for mercy. To drop back and punt. To say, “I give.” Or to cry, “uncle.” I was on the bottom of enough skirmishes and fights growing up, pinned helplessly on

[3] J. B. Phillips, *The New Testament in Modern English*, 385.

the ground, I learned to say it pretty easily.

As I said, I know some folks who are about to give up on their marriage. To give up fighting a painful or debilitating illness. To give up on ever being happy in life. To give up on life, on someone else. On getting well. On getting the right job, or just any job at all. On having children. Finding a suitable mate. There are people sitting around you today who have given up on any hope that there is someone out there who cares for them or who can help them. They've given up finding a friend or finding answers.

One of the ways I have been motivated to keep trying, to keep the faith, to hang in there, is reading the accounts of folks who met rejection and failure, but who went beyond it to success. Jim Valvano is also quoted as saying, "Never give up! Failure and rejection are only the first step to succeeding." He's right. Let me illustrate that.

I've done enough free-lance writing and submitting of manuscripts to know what it's like to be "rejected." That's why I take great comfort and encouragement from reminding myself that:

•Madeleine L'Engle's *A Wrinkle in Time* was rejected by 26 publishers before being accepted and going on to win a medal as the best children's book of 1963.
•Meg Cabot's *Princess Diaries* was rejected seventeen times.
•J. K. Rowling spent six years writing the first installment of her "Harry Potter" novels and it was rejected by 9 publishers.
•Stephen King got the following rejection for what would become a bestselling novel, *Carrie*, "We are not interested in science fiction which deals with negative utopias. They do not sell." After 30 rejections, King threw the manuscript into the trash. His wife fished it out and he decided to send it around again. Eventually, it was published.
•*The Diary of Anne Frank* was rejected 16 times before being published in 1952. More than 30 million copies are currently in print.
•Dr. Seuss books got rejected more than 15 times before the author finally found an editor who accepted his work.
•American literary great, William Saroyan, collected a pile of rejection slips thirty inches high—about 7000 of them—before he sold his first short story.
•Richard Hooker's book *M*A*S*H* was rejected 17 times.
•One publisher wrote to Rudyard Kipling, "You just don't know how to use the English language."
•The first book in the popular series, *Chicken Soup for the Soul*, was

rejected 140 times. The 65 books in the series have sold more than 80 million copies—in spite of the fact publishers said "anthologies don't sell" and the books were "too positive."
•Emily Dickinson had only 7 poems published during her lifetime.
•Margaret Mitchell's *Gone with The Wind* was rejected 38 times. It won the Pulitzer Prize in 1937. Don't you wonder what would have happened had she given up after 38 rejections?

What are the lessons we can take away from those examples? For one thing, they knew the difference between being knocked down and being knocked out. Also, it pays to be persistent. To persevere. To be patient. St. Paul put all three of them together and simply said "So we do not lose heart." And we don't give up.

My mother would always say, "Let nature take its course." I was startled to read that seeds of water lotus plants have germinated after more than a 1000 years of burial in the mud. One Canadian botanist reported that he found seeds of the Arctic Lupine that sprouted and grew healthy plants after about 10,000 years of preservation in frozen silt.

The key is always to hang on. Just a little longer. In rural South Alabama during the Great Depression, there was an outbreak of hog cholera. One Saturday afternoon a group of farmers were sitting in front of the country store discussing their situation. There was one old farmer who seemed to have had more experience than the others, so they turned to him for advice about what to expect. He thought for a moment and then made this encouraging pronouncement: "Hit appears that them what gits it and lingers for a few days do better than them what gits it and dies right off." Can you hang on a little longer? Can you linger a little longer?

Sometimes the best words we can think or utter are "not yet." Like the response of an 85-year-old woman who was asked if she had any children. She said, "Not yet!" The little word "yet" can make a big difference. It is one thing to say "I don't have it," but quite another to say "I don't have it *yet*." "I am not there," or "I am not there *yet*." God wants us to have that kind of forward-looking faith.

The Letter to the Hebrews tells us to "run with perseverance the race that is set before us" (Heb 12:1). Your doubts are not the end of the story. Your fears are not the end of the story. Your worries are not the end of the story. Your problems are not the end of the story. Your disappointments are not the end of the story. You've got to hang around long enough to see how the story ends.

I once heard someone say "No defeat is final unless you believe it to be." That attitude is illustrated profoundly by a reading of Abraham Lincoln's political career. He went to war a captain, and through no fault of his own, returned a private. He was a failure as a businessman. As a lawyer in Springfield, he was too impractical, too temperamental to be a success. He turned to politics and was defeated in his first try for the Legislature. He was defeated in his first attempt to be nominated for Congress. Defeated in his application to be Commissioner of the general Land Office. Defeated in the Senatorial Election of 1854. Defeated in his efforts for the Vice-presidency in 1856. Defeated again in the Senatorial Election of 1858. At about that time he wrote in a letter to a friend: "I am now the most miserable man living. If what I feel were equally distributed to the whole human family, there would not be one cheerful face on the earth." But, as Paul Harvey used to say, the rest of the story sees Abe Lincoln in the White House, in 1861.

A man by the name of Harlan lost his father when he was just five years old. They lived in southern Indiana, as a matter of fact. At fourteen, Harlan dropped out of school. He tried odd jobs as a farm hand and hated it. He tried being a streetcar conductor and hated that. At sixteen, he lied about his age and joined the Army—and hated that, too. He tried blacksmithing in Alabama and couldn't do it. He became a railroad locomotive fireman, liked it okay, got married at eighteen, and the day his wife said she was going to have a baby he was fired again. His wife left him. Then came the Depression. He tried studying law by correspondence and quit. He tried selling insurance, selling tires, running a ferryboat, running a filling station. He couldn't do any of that successfully. Much later in life he became chief cook and bottle washer in a restaurant in Corbin, Kentucky, but eventually the new highway bypassed the restaurant, and he was again out of a job. The years slid by. He had succeeded at nothing. On the day the postman brought him his first Social Security check, something within him went off. He would not have the government feeling sorry for him or looking after him. He didn't want to think the only thing he could do was retire. So, he got so angry he took the check for $105 and started a new business. The business he started with his first Social Security check was Kentucky Fried Chicken. The man who never really got started until it was about time to stop was Colonel Harlan Sanders.

Edwin Louis Cole once said, "You don't drown by falling in water, you drown by staying there." They used to say that a sermon should have three points and a poem. The poems come later, but here are my three points:

Point I: No failures ever need be final. The experience of failure is often the best teacher there is. The difference between those who ultimately succeed in life and those who do not is not that some avoid failure. No one can do that. The difference is that they don't give up.

Point II: The labels of failure are often false. Not only are there folks who give up; there are some *who are given up on*. I like the list of persons whom others gave up on. We not only give up; we give up on others. They were rejected by others. Thomas Edison was fired from his first two jobs for being "non-productive." Charlie Chaplin was rejected in Hollywood because his pantomime was considered "nonsense." Albert Einstein flunked out of school and was called "non-intelligent." Charles Schultz had every cartoon he submitted rejected by his high school yearbook staff. Henry Kissinger was remembered by his classmates as the kid nobody wanted to eat lunch with. A music teacher declared that his student, Beethoven, would "never write anything worthwhile." A Hollywood talent judge watched Fred Astaire's screen test and said, "Can't act. Can't sing. Can dance a little." Charles Darwin's father said he would be nothing more than a disgrace to his family. Walt Disney was fired by a newspaper editor because he "had no good ideas." Lou Gehrig was such a clumsy ball player that the boys in his neighborhood wouldn't let him play on their team.

No failure need be final. The labels of failure are often false.

Point III: Failure may well be the ground out of which success grows. Edison made 1,000 unsuccessful attempts at the light bulb. A reporter asked, "How did it feel to fail 1,000 times?" Edison replied, "I didn't fail 1,000 times. The light bulb was an invention with 1,000 steps." His friend Henry Ford was right when he said that failure was "the opportunity to begin again, more intelligently." When General Robert E. Lee was defeated at Gettysburg, he wrote to Jefferson Davis, "We must expect reverses, even defeats. They are sent to teach us wisdom and prudence, to call forth greater energies." A book on engineering has as its theme "the role of failure in successful design." It says that engineers learn "to make things that work by steadily improving upon things that did not work."

There is another arena in which we need to hear the encouraging word "Don't give up." Some of us have given our lives to working to change the world. At least making a difference. Some of us have committed ourselves to trying to be peacemakers. We have all prayed for peace. And it has not come. It's easy to shrug our shoulders and say, "What's the use? Nothing is ever any different." But there is a little story that may encourage us to keep going.

> It was deep winter and the snow was falling steadily upon the hillside. A tiny mouse crept out of its hole for a little break in its long winter sleep. Drowsily, the little mouse looked around and twitched its whiskers, and would have gone back to sleep inside its hole, had not a tiny voice echoed from somewhere out there in the white winter world. "Hello, little mouse. Can't you sleep?"
>
> The mouse looked around and caught sight of a tiny bird sitting, shivering on a barren branch just overhead. "Hello, Jenny Wren," said the mouse, pleased to find some company on this bleak day. "I just came up for a bit of air before I go back to sleep for the rest of the winter."
>
> But it was so good to find company that for a while the mouse and the wren sat there together, huddled beneath the lowest branches of a pine tree, watching the snow falling and enjoying a little congenial conversation.
>
> "How much do you think a snowflake weighs?" the mouse asked the wren suddenly.
>
> "A snowflake weighs almost nothing," the wren replied. "A snowflake is so insignificant; it carries almost no weight at all. How could you possibly weigh a snowflake?"
>
> "Oh, I disagree," said the mouse. "In fact, I can tell you that last winter, around this time, I woke up from my winter dreaming and came out for a breath of fresh air, and because I had no companions and nothing better to do, I sat here counting the snowflakes as they fell. I watched them settling on these branches and covering the pine needles with a blanket of whiteness. I got as far as two million, four hundred and ninety-two thousand, three hundred and fifty-nine. And then…when the very next snowflake fell and settled on the branch—the branch dropped right down to the ground and all the snow slid off. So, a snowflake does weigh something. It does make a difference!"
>
> The wren, who was only a tiny little bird herself and didn't think she had much influence on the great big world around her, pondered for a long time over the mouse's story. "Perhaps," she thought to

herself, “it really is true that just one little voice can make a difference.”[4]

So, don’t give up. You may be that last snowflake.

I realize there is a lot of "but on the other hand" in this chapter, but there is a difference between a second chance and a last chance. Not everything can be put off indefinitely. We do not have unlimited opportunities, countless days, endless chances. The farmer's hired hand, after all, had to say, "If the fig tree bears fruit next year, well and good; but if not, you can cut it down." It's as the poet Edwin Markham’s “The Day and the Work” puts it:

To each man is given a day and his work for the day:
And once, and no more, he is given to travel this way.

We "only go 'round once," to be sure. Let an anonymous poem illustrate for us the danger in saying "wait'll next year" too often:

Around the corner I have a friend
In this great city that has no end;
Yet days go by, and weeks rush on,
And before I know it a year has gone
And I never see my old friend's face,
For life is a swift and terrible race.
He knows I like him just as well
As in the days I rang his bell,
And he rang mine. We were younger then,
And now we're busy, tired men;
Tired with playing a foolish game,
Tired with trying to make a name.
“Tomorrow,” I say, “I'll call on Jim,
Just to show that I'm thinking of him.”
But tomorrow comes, and tomorrow goes,
And the distance between us grows and grows.
Around the corner--and yet miles away...
“Here's a message, sir...Jim died today.”
And that's what we get, and deserve in the end--

[4] Source Unknown, *One Hundred Wisdom Stories*, Margaret Silf, (ed.), (United Kingdom: Lion, 2011), 63-64.

Around the corner, a vanished friend.[5]

How tragic is the number of letters never written, of phone calls not made, of "I'm sorrys" or "I love yous" never expressed--simply because we foolishly believe there will always be time. As all sorts of invitations are extended to us, many of us respond with, "Maybe next year; wait'll next year." I cannot help but wonder if "next year" will ever arrive for them.

There was a notice on the wall of the garden store that said, "The best time to plant a tree was twenty-five years ago. The second-best time is today." The parable Jesus told ends without our knowing if the additional year and enriched soil did any good. In the same way, we'll have to wait to see if this book did any good for you. Will we have to wait till next year, or will you do something about it today?

Is there something you want to do, need to do? Don't wait'll next year. Do it now.

Questions for Contemplating and Conversing

1. Are you a procrastinator? About what things?
2. What have you put-off doing that you should do as soon as possible?
3. How many of the things on your To-do List should be done *now*?
4. Have you ever given up too soon?
5. Do you have a "not yet" attitude in life?
6. When has it been wise for you to wait?
7. What is the main lesson you learned from this chapter?

[5] Charles Hanson Towne, *A World of Windows and Other Poems*, (New York: George H. Doran Company, 1919), 66.